Economics for Beginners

Everything You Need to Know About Economics

(A Complete Guide for Beginners on How to Invest Properly)

Briana Markham

Published By **Bella Frost**

Briana Markham

All Rights Reserved

Economics for Beginners: Everything You Need to Know About Economics (A Complete Guide for Beginners on How to Invest Properly)

ISBN   978-1-77485-868-4

No part of this guidebook shall be reproduced in any form without permission in writing from the publisher except in the case of brief quotations embodied in critical articles or reviews.

Legal & Disclaimer

The information contained in this ebook is not designed to replace or take the place of any form of medicine or professional medical advice. The information in this ebook has been provided for educational & entertainment purposes only.

The information contained in this book has been compiled from sources deemed reliable, and it is accurate to the best of the Author's knowledge; however, the Author cannot guarantee its accuracy and validity and cannot be held liable for any errors or omissions. Changes are periodically made to this book. You must consult your doctor or get professional medical advice before using any of the suggested remedies, techniques, or information in this book.

Upon using the information contained in this book, you agree to hold harmless the Author from and against any damages, costs, and expenses, including any legal fees potentially resulting from the application of any of the information provided by this guide. This disclaimer applies to any damages or injury caused by the use and application, whether directly or indirectly, of any advice or information presented, whether for breach of contract, tort, negligence, personal injury, criminal intent, or under any other cause of action.

You agree to accept all risks of using the information presented inside this book. You need to consult a professional medical practitioner in order to ensure you are both able and healthy enough to participate in this program.

TABLE OF CONTENTS

Introduction

The term "economy" refers to the social science that's goal is to explain all aspects that affect the distribution, production, and use of certain products and services. Naturally, not all people are an expert in economics. But we live in an age where some level of knowledge in economics is required for anyone who wants to be more productive or understand what's happening around the globe because economics affect all aspects of our lives. This book can help anyone who is interested in learning more about economics, for whatever reason. Looking online for answers isn't efficient as results are or are not reliable or too complex for us to grasp.

This book will teach you everything about the economy, from the early days of economic thought up to the present-day economy. You will discover what the contemporary economy has been adept at dealing with the issue of scarcity. You will also be taught the basic terms in economics that you've heard before but didn't know what they mean.

In addition, the section is devoted to trading. It is more than buying a product and then paying fees for it. With the right strategy, trade can turn to be a success or even break your bank. What is the answer whether to trade or not trade can be found inside this guide.

Have you ever wondered whether the world's economy is expanding, or if it's slowing down? Find this book out what's really happening and what government can do to boost the economy.

If you've ever wondered why there's not enough money. It's simple to print more money, wouldn't it? But that's not feasible. This book will assist you in understanding money and will teach you all you can about inflation. Since inflation is a real threat, it can cause financial crises and recession. Additionally, you will understand the basics of recession: what it is, the causes behind it, the causes as well as the effects and prevention strategies.

Chapter 1 Economic: How Humans And

Societies Deal With Scarcity

Have you ever considered what your life could be like if we were able to have everything you could ever want? Imagine if, with just one swipe we could obtain the things we want when we need it, like cash to purchase clothing, food, shelter and other gadgets? You'd have more time to do whatever you want. The reality of life is that resources are limited, and many people need or desire the same things as you do.

Economics, being an aspect of Social Sciences, deal with the needs and desires of a person against the resources that are available to him. Economics, as a social science subject to the word"economics"came via an Greek word"oikonomia" which was derived in the two words,"oikos"meaning"house and"nemein"meaning manager. Literally it means"house manager."Here is a list of definitions for economics derived from various sources:

* Antonioni and Flynn define Economics as the field of study which studies how

individuals as well as societies, generally make choices that allow them to maximize the value from their resources.

* Funk and Wagnalls Encyclopedia states that Economics as a social science is concerned with the distribution, production, exchange and consumption of goods and services. The Economist studies the manner people, or groups, be it businesses or government institutions strive to reach whatever economic goal they choose.

* Economics is the social science concerned with the effective utilization of scarce resources to maximize satisfaction for the needs of the economy.

Studying Economics begins by knowing how scarcity works as well as opportunities cost. The idea of scarcity is that there aren't enough resources available to satisfy every person's desires. It occurs when the amount that people desire is greater than the amount of resources available. People are always hungry. No matter how much or little they are always looking for something. Because a person is limited in resources and time, he must determine what he desires most and ignore the rest. What they choose to do as well as the method by the way they make these choices will tell you why the current world is the way it is currently.

This leads us back to the idea of the concept of. Due to limited resources or scarcity, an individual must choose between several options. If he chooses one it means he has to give up other options. The economists describe the lost advantages of the next-best alternative as the opportunity cost or the best-valued option that is sacrificed in the event of a decision being made. As with individuals, societies have to make daily choices due to the limited resources. Society must make compromises when they decide to allocate only a small amount of resources to meet one desire in the absence of the other. For instance, when you download this ebook you have to choose between having it read now or later or perhaps watching TV. This is the choice between taking it up now and taking economics classes or watching television.

Generally, economists research the ways that individuals and societies manage the issue of scarcity.

To grasp the idea of Economics in a holistic manner, economists typically divide the study of Economics into two broad categories which are Microeconomics and Macroeconomics. We will explore more deeply these subjects, however, for the moment, here's the basic definition:

It is the study of the economic system as a whole. Themes, like growth in the national economy as well as inflation, government spending and unemployment are all discussed under macroeconomics. As per Antonioni as well as Flynn, Macroeconomics also encompasses the analysis of economic growth and the way governments use fiscal or monetary policy to combat recessions.

* Microeconomics: this refers to the analysis of smaller economic units, like firms, individuals or even industries. Consumer spending, labor markets as well as personal decision-making is covered under microeconomics as well. Antonioni as well as Flynn Microeconomics describe how people make decisions regarding which place to spend money or put savings into. The book also describes how companies react when they compete in different markets.

A Short Introduction to the History of Economic Thought

As a newcomer to the field of Economics it is essential to be aware of the various types of thought or theories that influence the way we view economics and economics in the present.

Free Market Thought (late medieval and early modern Europe)

In a market that is free price is determined through a non-coerced, mutual consensus between buyers and sellers and the government is not able to control the demand and supply of these goods. It is believed that the participants are not manipulating prices or mislead investors when they are in a market that is free. The opposite of an open market is a regulated market. The government determines and regulates prices directly or regulates demand and supply in controlled markets. However, the ideal of a market is not actually a reality in actual reality. In reality there is price fixing or manipulation and some people do not make trades on their own.

Mercantilism (from the period 16th - 18th century)

The economic theory which declares that the prosperity of a country is dependent on its capital resources and that the overall amount of trade that it has is variable. The assets of an economic nation are represented through bullion such as silver or gold, which is held by the government. Mercantilism theory supports notion of balance of trade between import and export. The government should encourage exports and deter imports to improve capital and balance trade.

Classical Economics (around 1776)

Adam Smith's The Wealth of Nation, is widely considered to be the birth in the field of Classical Economics. The theory of economics is thought as the first school modern in economics. In addition to Smith, David Ricardo, Thomas Malthus and John Stuart Mill are thought to be the main supporters of this perspective. Classical Theorists of economics attempted to clarify the notion of development and growth. Economic goals are viewed as a matter of interest in the form of class, not the kings or rulers. It's a gradual transition from feudal to market-based capitalism.

Laissez-faire Economics (19th century-around 1867)

As a relic of free market thinking in conjunction with Classical Economics, laissez-faire economics advocates the view that governments are not allowed to interfere with markets. The state is not legally under obligation to interfere or ensure equal distribution of wealth or to establish an welfare state that protects people from being in poverty. Laissez-faire literally refers to"let do"or"let the situation be."

A belief system that ensures private production and enterprises are expected to be unaffected from state intervention. They will grow and prosper more if they were left to their own rules.

Neoclassical Economics (1871-1877)

The principle of demand and supply develops into the main theme of neoclassical economics. Prices, outputs and the distribution of income in market are affected by supply and demand. It is possible to achieve a maximum of income, governed by individuals , and of the costs-constrained profits for firms.

Keynesean Economic Theory (1921 from 1921 to)

John Maynard Keynes, in his most influential book, discussed the importance of government in the economic. In his General Theory of Employment, Interest, and Money, Keynes envisioned a reformation of capitalism or a managed one. Keynes spoke of an economy that is unstable, and a classical economists, as being incorrect to believe that demand and supply will guarantee complete employment. The policies that govern the economy of today are based on Keynes economic theories. The macroeconomics theory draws a lot of its basic ideas from Keynes for example, the way that fiscal policy is used by government such as deficit, spending and taxation.

"Trickle-down" Economics (1981)

It is usually associated with the theory of supply-side economics that claims that a reduction in taxes related to capital gains income from corporations, as well as other high personal income will lead to more business investment as well as economic expansion. According to this theory those who otherwise have to pay taxes will be able to distribute the benefits to those who are less rich and, consequently, boost the economy. The assumptions behind trickle-down economics proved to be faulty, as the savings generated by taxes and other levies aren't dispersed to the entire population.

Natural Capitalism (1990's)

The increasing threat of devastation of the natural environment in the name of capitalism led to the way for a more long-lasting economics. Natural Capitalism establishes standards and introduces reforms that reward the efficiency of energy and materials when exploiting market systems. It advocates ecological harmony and eco-friendly practices to expand the use of natural capital.

Due to the scarcity of resources, every society has to be able to answer these three questions about economics:

* What kind of goods or services are required to be manufactured?

How are they to be created?

* Who is the person who would use these products and services?

The way that societies address these questions will determine the kind of system of economics they want to establish. An economic system according to economists is the way that society employs to produce and distribute products and services. There are generally two kinds of economic systems: the centrally planned economy or command economy as well as an open market system. A few economists also suggested another economic system that is a mix of free market and command economy.

* In a Centrally planned or command economy the government controls all production factors and decides what it will produce and how much. The government also decides who will be the recipients of the products and services.

The free market system is based on a laxity, where the government has very little or nothing to the economy. A private or individual group are the sole owners of the elements of production. Self-interest and competition act like the"invisible hand"in the marketplace. They are the regulators of the market economy that is free.

In a mixed economic system, the government is able to regulate economic activities as private individuals and groups are able to own resources and create products and services. It's a hybrid of centrally planned economies and a free market economy. Today, most societies have mixed economies.

Chapter 2: Use Of Scarce Resources To

Maximize Happiness

Let's begin this chapter by examining some fundamental economic assumptions:

1. Societies and individuals have endless desires. However the resources available are all limited in terms of shortage.

2. Due to limited resources there are a lot of choices to be made. Each decision made there is a concept of cost of trade-off and the opportunity cost.

3. Everyone is keen on making choices that maximize their satisfaction."Self-interest"motivates everyone's actions.

4. People think and make decisions through comparing marginal costs and marginal advantages of each possible option.

5. The real world can be modeled and analysed by using simple diagrams and graphs.

The fundamental assumptions mentioned above are crucial when deciding how to effectively make use of the resources available to achieve the greatest happiness or benefit. Economics see the following as resources:

* Land is not just the geographic physical land. For economists, it includes all naturally occurring sources, which could be utilized to make products that people would like to consume.

* Labor is the process of putting in work or input of humans to create items. For instance, flour will not turn into bread without the intervention of humans.

* Capital - These are created by the human being, and are not consumed directly, but are used to create other products. They could be tools, equipment, or other types of structures.

Economic analysts also refer to the above mentioned resources factors, or inputs, of production. Some economists of today also consider Human Capital as an input or resource. It is the information or abilities that people typically use to create an output.

To show the flow of income and resources:

Owners of the components of production or resources like labor, land and capital, can rent or sell them to others to create products, including products and services. The income would be from rent for the use of land as well as wage for labor or interest to use capital. The owners of resources have the ability to purchase goods using the earnings they earn from the use or sale their resource. However the manufacturers of goods make money by selling their products, thus having the capacity to buy or pay rent or use of the resources they use to create outputs.

How do we know what they can produce and what resources to use to increase happiness for humans? The economist identifies a two-step procedure that follows:

1. Every society has to figure out the best possible combinations of outputs that it can create in the context of its resources and the technology available in the present.

2. The society must select among the options available the one that will bring maximum happiness.

It is possible to measure success by the degree of efficiency achieved by two methods. These are:

a. Productive efficiency is the process of producing items and services with the smallest amount of resources.

B. Allocative efficiency, the production of products and services that make people feel most content and in enough of them in the right quantity.

Economic analysts determine what is feasible to create in an economy by identifying two main elements. These variables affect the amount and type of outputs that can be produced: limited resources and declining returns.

Naturally, if resources are infinite, there's no reason to decide what products to create, since products and services will be infinite. Some others, however are unable to grasp how to diminish returns. The less more you produce of the item or product and services, the lower return you receive for each unit. In the end, the price of manufacturing the item or services outweighs the benefits that would reduce the amount of production. The limited resources and the diminishing profits define the possibilities of production.

One of the tools used by Economists to clarify concepts and understand circumstances is the use of graphs and models. A good example of this kind of graphical design is known as that of the Production Possibilities Curve expressed in the form of a Production Possibilities Graph (PPG). The graph illustrates every possibilities of combining two goods that a society might create, given a finite amount and the high quality resources. PPG can graphically depict opportunities cost, scarcity potential tradeoffs, as well as even the efficiency of production of services and goods. There are four main assumptions that are based on this graphic model:

1. Two products are made.

2. The resources are fully utilized.

3. They are also fixed resource.

4. There are certain technologies that must be fixed.

Here's an example of the Production Possibilities Curve:

The graph represents the possible production of butter and guns. By looking at the the points C, B D B, D and C and C, we can see they're in the middle of the curve. It shows the efficiency of using resources to create the goods. Point X on the contrary, indicates an unattainable output with the current technology or capital available, or both. Point A is located beneath the curve, which illustrates the under-utilization of production capacity. As per economists, shifts in the PPC could occur when there is an improvement in the production factors. It could happen in the event that there the growth in capital, or when better technology is readily available. Productivity efficiency is shown on the PPC where the points are within the range of the curve. Social efficiency is achieved when goods are manufactured according to the needs of the population.

Chapter 3: To Trade Or Not To Trade It Is The

Issue.

As we have discussed that the study of economics can be studied by analyzing the whole economy in macroeconomics or microeconomics. Microeconomics is the study of how firms or individuals determine how they allocate their limited resources, what they will produce, and to whom to make it. Microeconomics studies how the various combinations of these options and the actions that lead to these choices affect the supply and demand of products and services. This is then going to influence the price of the goods. The price is then a factor in the quantity of demand and supply of both goods and services.

In the preceding chapter, we examined the different sources used to create products and services. Because of the limited supply, individuals and companies must decide which products to make and how they will consume the products or services created. Be aware that there's always a trade-off to consider when choosing one option over the other.

Also, there is an expense to consider when choosing one option over the alternative.

Consider the following table as an example:

Table 1 lists the two jobs Mary and Joe are able to accomplish, given the time frame. Let's believe that we can expect identical quality from their output. The only difference is in the amount of output. If, for instance, Mary commits 100% of her time, and an hour is allotted to Math issues, she will complete 10 tasks in just an hour, but she is not competent to solve any Science issues. The potential cost of solving 10 math-related problems in one hour Mary is the 10 science tasks she could have completed instead. Joe is in contrast, can solve 10 math problems within an hour however only five science-related problems in about the same time. If he is spending all his time solving math-related problems, he'll complete 10 problems which is at the expense of five science-related problems. The opportunity cost of solving 10 math problems is five science-related problems.

How do the cost of opportunity and specialization, comparative advantage, and trade connect to each other in the above example?

First, let's imagine that Mary Joe and Mary Joe decide to share their resources for the production of both of their products. In this case they will have one hour. Their products provide solutions to mathematics and science-related issues.

In an hour, Mary can do 5 math and five science-related questions. Joe is able to solve five math problems, but only 2.5 science issues. The outputs they produce when working together are combined to create 10 math problems , and 7.5 science-related issues.

Our hypothetical subjects observe that they can probably use their resources effectively and achieve more effective results if they collaborate rather than work alone. The next question is which one would be the most productive, using the identical resources? The answer is in the one with less risk of losing money when selecting one option in comparison to the alternative. Let's go back to our previous example. It is evident on the chart that Mary can handle science and math equally and can solve science tasks more efficiently than Joe could. However, Joe's chance cost for only doing Math problems is lower in comparison to Mary who is specialized in math-related problems.

In this way, Joe has a comparative advantage in math because Joe would have a lower chance cost than Mary in the event that he chooses to only solve math-related problems. If Mary is a specialist in Math then she will have to offer up a science-related problem for every math challenge she tackles within one hour. On the other hand Mary has an advantage in science because her chance cost is less that Joe is. If Joe is able to spend his time on science-related work, he'll lose 2 maths problems, while Mary just loses 1. The lower cost of opportunity and the competitive advantage is now the basis for specificization.

Once we've established that we benefit from specialization in the production of certain services and products when we can lower our chance cost, and this is where the idea of trade becomes relevant.

Reviewing our scenario. Imagine that Mary and Joe made the decision to trade their products. What is the best scenario?

Mary will solve all questions in science in an hour. She will exchange one science for each math answer from Joe. As she is able to complete 10 science questions in one hour, she suggests one-to-one exchange. In the final result, Mary will get 5 math solutions and five science solutions. This scenario for trading will grant Joe the opportunity to earn 2.5 gain from trading, as if he can complete everything in an hour, he will only tackle 2.5 science-related issues.

Take another look at a trading scenario.

In the event that Mary insists on receiving 2 math solutions to every Science trade Joe is only able to receive 2.5 science solutions, as Joe only has five mathematics problems in exchange. Mary has 7.5 Science solutions in an hour. In this case, Mary will have 2.5 gain from trading with Joe.

The benefit of trading is the benefits both parties receive that is higher than the output each would have made in the absence of trade or had they been working independently. In every scenario of trading each party gains something through the transaction, otherwise, they could not be able to trade in any way at all. This is the case all the time in reality. The phenomenon of specializing and trading occurs because everyone always wants or needs more than they're in a position to create. Through specializing and trading companies and individuals maximize their resources to create the most value or satisfaction. This is the fundamental assumption in Economics. People act in ways that provide them with the most benefits or highest happiness given the resources they are given. People are more likely to trade when they realize that giving up something can provide them with a lower opportunity cost and a higher comparative advantage and greater gains from trading. That is that if the advantage of trading (gain) is greater than the expense of making an exchange, trading is likely to occur.

Let's summarize what we've learned so far:

1. Some people choose to exchange or trades since they believe that the gains outweighs the expense of exchange. Also, exchanges can be beneficial for both the parties.

2. Making a decision on which option to choose is based on chance cost, which is the amount of one unit of service or good that is

sacrificed in order to obtain the benefit of the same product or service.

3. In the field of specialization, an individual or firm or the entire nation will consider its cost of opportunity. You are specialized in an area with the lowest chance cost.

4. Through the specialization and trade, people or firms and even nations can obtain more of the items they need , than were they able to produce it on their own. It is beneficial to trade in the case of activities that which you can perform more effectively than the competition.

Chapter 4: Does The Economy Grow Or

Slowing Down?

Have you heard of the term first world nation? Have you wondered whether your country is a third world nation? Have you had a conversation with the word "developing" nation? What is the method used by economists to classify nations? What are the underlying factors of how they conduct their business?

As we have discussed in previous chapters that the distribution and production of services and goods is carried out by businesses or individuals within the capitalist system of economics or by the government within the command economy. Many of our current economic systems are a mixture of centrally planned economies as well as markets that are free. The study of the production and distribution of services and goods based on scarce resources and taking an analysis of the entire economy is a part of Macroeconomics. Economics researchers devise strategies to comprehend and monitor the resources used and the goods created through a massive accounting system that tracks the economic activity. This is known as National Accounts or, internationally, National Income and Product accounts (NIPA). The system of accounts cranks out a variety of important data, like GDP, or Gross Domestic Product. The GDP measures the country's total production of goods and services during a specific time. It is typically expressed as an increase or decrease in percentage from the previous period of reporting. When you read or hear that GDP has increased by four percent, it is indicating that the economy increased by 4% over previous year.

There are two methods to measure GDP. It is possible to measure it by adding up all expenditures for purchasing goods and services, or by adding each income from the production of products and services. These numbers ought to make sense. The equation in algebraic terms looks like this:

It is C + C + C + C + C + C +

Where:

Y - is the gross domestic product during that time

C = Consumption-these are the total of all expenditures that households make for items and services, regardless of whether they are locally or imported. Consumption is a component of disposable or after-tax incomes for households. Simply put, if you have a higher disposable income, you will have more money to spend on items and services, in the event that you do not have to save it all. The tax policies of governments also affect consumption. Tax policies affect the amount of disposable income, as well as the people's tendency to spend or save.

I = investment - these are expenses made to purchase new capital expenditures, such as factories, or even equipment. They also include inventories and products that are manufactured but not yet sold in the period of the report. It is crucial to know what amount a business will invest to ensure the smooth running of economic activity. Businesses invest or purchase capital to create products and services. There must be a reason for business owners to keep purchasing capital or investing in capital to create. However, depreciation can occur in the event that capital breaks down or is obsolete or even thrown away. Depreciation lowers your capital stocks. Any investment that is greater than depreciation increases the total amount of stock, which results in more outputs that people are able to consume.

What can a businessperson do in deciding whether to invest capital? The answer is found in comparing two variables. The factors to consider are:

1. Potential benefits are measured in potential profits.

2. The cost of capital acquisition measured as interest rates. It is not important whether or not a business decides to take loans to purchase capital.

If you're thinking of saving money or taking out the need for a loan, one the first questions you need to consider what is your interest rates. The interest rate influences the flow of economic activity by encouraging businesses and individuals to invest capital in the production of products or services, or to loan the money to other people. When a business requires capital to run its production but isn't able to pay for it the company may have to resort to borrowing. A higher interest rate on loans means greater payments. The business might have second opinions of investing money into an economy in this scenario. If the business is able to afford capital, it might require a decision between cash for the purchase of equipment or lending cash to other businesses. If the company is paying a high interest rate, it's more appealing to lend the cash.

To help stabilize the market, certain government officials intervene to set interest rates. The government can decide to set rates lower or higher, according to the economic conditions. In the event that the country is struggling government could lower interest rates in order to encourage companies to invest in their businesses and help in improving the economy.

G is the term used to describe government. It stands for the expenditures of the government on current produced items and services, and is not the exchange of funds of one party to the next. How does the government obtain money to buy products and services? It receives money from taxes as well as borrowing. A government is able to balance its budget when its expenditures are in line with tax revenue. If the tax revenues are higher than the expenses and the government is in an surplus in its budget. If tax revenues are greater than expenditures and the government is in an unsustainable budget. Since a government has to continue to function, even when it is running an unsustainable budget that is why it borrows through the market for financial. In the calculation of GDP, it doesn't matter how or where the government allocates its funds. What is important for economists when calculating an estimate of GDP, is just how tiny or large the amount of expenditure is dependent on the variables that were taken into consideration when the calculation of the amount.

They are financial instruments utilized by the government to borrow money. When a government needs to borrow money they sell bond to the investors. Investors earn money from purchasing these bonds as the government pays the interest on the bonds.

Net export = NX - this is the total of a country's exports plus the imports.

The sale of products or services to a business or an individual from another country is referred to as exports , or EX in economics. If a person in the country you reside in purchases something in another country, this is known as imports or the term IM. When calculating GDP, net exports, also known as NX, is the total worth of the exports, minus everything else that was imported in the time. When the method of expenditure is employed to calculate GDP, the net export , also known as NX is included in the equation of GDP. If a country is able to have greater exports than it imports, it is a surplus in trade. In the opposite case, if the import is greater than export then the country is considered to be experiencing a trade deficit.

Do you recall our discussion on trade from earlier chapters? Trade is a way to make the most efficient use of their scarce resources. The goal is about achieving the maximum satisfaction using the resources available or production factors. It is also true for those who trade with other nations. The international trade market has proven to be an important economic driver over the last years. Countries trade with one another as there are not enough resources in each nation to meet their own citizens' needs and desires. There are naysayers who those who oppose trade with other countries shiver when they hear the words the trade deficit or surplus. When people hear terms like deficit and surplus in the context of trade, they have powerful implications that can suggest that surpluses are more beneficial than deficits, which economists do not approve.

Through global trade has become one global market. There are those who oppose globalization and trade use the term surplus or deficit and believes that only one side gets the benefits of trade. As the international trade is free of charge, then every trade made will increase or increase satisfaction. Both parties are happy because of their trades, even though on paper one appears having more wealth than another. It is important to keep in mind is the way they arrange their wealth and assets in the aftermath of a voluntary trade will make them happier.

For instance, Eric has $100 and 50 apples. Linda has 100 fifty oranges. Oranges and apples cost one dollar. Eric would like to purchase 30 oranges for $30 , and Linda is looking to purchase 20 apple for just $20. At the conclusion of the exchange, Eric has $70, 20 apples and 30 oranges and Linda has $80, 20 oranges , and 20 apples. After removing all the goods that result from the exchange, Eric is left with $70 and Linda is left with $80.

If we just see money in trade then we could conclude that Eric received the lower end of the deal, while Linda received more. We must not forget that when we trade, we consider every resource and output that result from the participation of the trade partners. Additionally, we need to recognize that each of the parties was willing to follow the requirements of the trade. Although Eric only had $70, he's really happy, as the trade brought him 30 oranges the exchange, which can't be made by him due to his insufficient resources. Linda was also happy thanks to the trade. She got 20 apples through the trade. If they didn't trade the apples, they would each have $100 , and they would have only their own produce. However, they'd also be depressed as they wouldn't be able enhance their product and hence their joy. A diet of only apples or oranges is boring, isn't it?

The GDP equation may not be completely accurate, because it is possible that other situations cannot be accounted for like the underground economy or those that don't disclose their earnings or consumption such as those in rural households However, economists find the GDP report to be beneficial in analyzing the macroeconomic performance of a nation. Every indicator indicates a shift within the overall economy of a country that is the determinant of growth or decline.

Why is it crucial to comprehend and calculate GDP in economics?

For economists, the GDP represents the total production of the economy for a particular country. It is the most frequently cited indicator of economics that reveals the most about the overall economic performance of a nation. Analysts, policy makers, and investors are all concerned about the country's GDP since it could indicate an increase in the economy or a recession. If the GDP is in the positive range is a sign of a strong economy. If businesses expand and demand for jobs increases, so too does the need for jobs. If employees are hired, they'll have the money to buy products and services, and this cycle will continue. If the economy slows down, businesses will not be able to create goods and services and could also cut back on employees. The higher unemployment rate affects the consumption and income of workers.

GDP between 2.5-3.5 percent per year is believed to be the most suitable range that will bring the highest economic advantages. It's good for businesses as it increases profits and job growth. However, it's secure enough to shield against inflation-related worries. A negative GDP over at least two quarters consecutively, as per experts, is a signal of a recession in the economy.

GNP, or Gross National Product, or GNP is a different economic indicator that is linked to GDP. However, instead of accounting for all the economic activities in the country It only counts the ones that are derived from workers and property within the limits of the country. The best comparability or index to show the production of an economy is the real GDP. This is more accurate, since it shows the fluctuating price of services and goods, that are calculated in terms of money. Also, it accounts for the effects of inflation and fluctuations in currency rates. Economic analysts base the Real GDP on a fixed unit of value which is typically in currency units in the year in question.

The expression of economic growth or decline as real GDP is much better than nominal GDP due to its higher accuracy in reporting consumption or production performance.

For instance, if Country A has an annual nominal GDP of $ 100 billion during 2000, and later reports an actual GDP of $150 billion in the year 2010 It is evident that the economy expanded in the time frame. But, using real GDP to gauge growth, between 2000 and the year 2010, the amount of dollar decreased by 50% as a result of currency fluctuations and inflation. Therefore, if we declare $150 billion using the rates of 2000, it could seem that the real GDP in 2010 was only $75 billion. Instead of expanding in 2010, the economy actually declined in the reporting period.

If you've got an understanding of the importance of GDP reports to determine the country's economic development or decline, the next sections will help anyone new to studying economics comprehend why countries don't make money though they have the technology to print it.

Chapter 5: What's The Reason? Can't An Administration Print More Money To Give To The Poor?

I can recall a story that occurred when I was an infant. There was a kid who demanded an increase in his money amount from his parents in order to purchase more candy. His parents were not wealthy and told him that they had to earn some money first before granting his requests. As a child, the first thing did he did was create a model of a dollar bill to present him to his parents. He explained that, today, they have the money to purchase what they require.

You might be amused by the absurdity of this incident, but the the dollar bill amount to nothing, as you could say. What happens if the federal state, in all its authority and power print additional money, and then distributes the proceeds to citizens specifically for those who are struggling and in need? Would that be considered legal if the government prints it? What happens to the economy? Would this have an impact on the economy of your country? Have you considered the current state of international trade and markets if this occurs? If the government print more money and then uses it to create the international market, then what changes would happen to the world economy? To answer the question asked I'll present another economy indicator which is popular nowadays, which is Inflation. Economics experts use the term Inflation to refer to a state within the economy in which prices in general is increasing. It is defined as the percentage of increase over the previous year. This doesn't necessarily mean that every single thing in the economy goes upwards, but the general trend is upwards when the economy is experiencing inflation.

If your grandparents tell you the story of how a loaf bread was only $1 during their youth, and an espresso in an expensive restaurant cost only $0.50 and the cost of a ride for a trip to the metro was just $1.25 and that's why you can attribute inflation for the price increase in the present. Every dollar you make can, for instance, cost you less in products and services due to the impact of inflation.

What is the cause of Inflation?

For a long time, economists debated on the reasons why inflation takes place. One of the widely acknowledged theories of inflation is Demand-Pull Inflation. Another theory is known as the Cost-Push Inflation.

In the case of the Demand-Pull Inflation The reason behind increasing prices or a condition in which inflation occurs is due to the quantity of money in the market that increases too fast. If a government distributes more money on the market and then distributes the cash to individuals, they will have more money to purchase items and services. If the producers of the goods and services are not producing at the speed that demand demands the prices will rise. Consumers are inclined to purchase the item, even at a greater pricebecause they are able to spend more. If businesses earn more from customers, they are able to produce more. When demand exceeds the supply of goods, companies tend to increase prices in order to keep up with demand, even though they continue to produce products. This cycle will continue indefinitely as long as there's more money than the products available for purchase. In order to prevent rising inflation, the increase of the money supply must be reduced. In the real world, with real politics, it cannot be easy to achieve.

Cost-Push Inflation - on the other hand, there's another situation where businesses want to improve their profits, despite costs of production increasing which is why they raise the cost of their products. Cost of production increases could be due to a variety of sources, like an the increase in taxes, wages for employees or the increased costs for imports.

Before proceeding I'll discuss the importance of money in the economic system.

In the past there was a system of bartering for items and services. In the case of example when I owned a cow and needed to purchase two sacks wheat grains, I would have find someone else willing to exchange the cow I had for two bags grains. This is a good thing and can be very effective when you find an individual who is willing to exchange with you within the shortest length of time. What will happen if I come across someone who would like my cow however, he doesn't possess two bags of wheat grain. Instead, he's got one barrel filled with beer. Then, I come across a person who is looking for to get a barrel of beer for two sacks worth of wheat grains. In order to obtain the things I want two sacks of wheat grain in exchange for a cow, I have to first trade with the proprietor of the beer barrel before negotiating in the name of the farmer who has the grain. Through this process I took longer to organize the trades. As we all know, time is also a scarce resource.

In the real world, that the economy has become to be so complex and large bartering has turned into an extremely tedious procedure. What is the solution? It's a matter of having a kind of a currency that everyone on the market can accept. In the above example I don't have to establish transactions between the beer maker and the owner of the grain to swap my cows for grains. Money becomes the means through which I can purchase grains from their owner. Money can be used as a way for trade to take place regardless of whether you don't own the commodity that a trader is looking for. It is a recognized method that can be used to pay for products and services.

What is the basis for determining the value of money? How can we determine what is the correct amount for trading with items and services? This is a question that lies within demand and supply of money.

In every economy it is the government that controls the quantity of money on the market. It can print even more, if it chooses to. The reason for the demand is its utility and as it is a means of exchange. Being able to have money does not mean needing to barter. If there is a shortage of money supply, people may use bartering as we have found out is an extremely tedious process. The value of money is now increased. If there's plenty of money floating around and bartering becomes less difficult and every amount of money is devalued in value as a means of exchange. A seller of goods could be able to get a better price for his goods in the event that he has an abundance of money. The prices of services and goods are proportional in relation to value for money.

In an economy that is growing the production of goods and other services rises, and customers need more money to purchase items that are available on the market. If this happens then the reaction of the government to the growing demand for money could result in one or more of the following situations:

1. If the demand for money is rising and the government print extra money, at the exact time in response to the rising demands, the worth of the currency does not change. Prices will also not change.

2. If the government printed additional money at greater rate than the demand for money, then inflation could take place. Each coin is deemed to be less valued. Due to its declining value it is necessary to have more of it to purchase items, which leads to rising prices for items and services.

3. In the event that the central bank prints currency less than the demand for money this causes inflation. You'll need less money to purchase items and services.

Have you ever wondered how economists determine how much inflation a government could expect when it creates more money? This theory of Quantity Theory of Money addresses this question. The theory says that the amount of prices in the marketplace is comparable to the amount of money in the market. That is that if you increase the money that circulates on the market, then the price of both goods and services will be also double.

If the prices of goods rise or if the cause of inflation is the government print excessive amounts of money, then what is the reason for it in the first instance? Three scenarios can provide the explanation for why governments adopt this decision:

1. In the event that the government isn't able to collect enough revenue from taxes to meet its obligations It may turn to printing additional money.

2. If the government is feeling the pressure of debtors who wish to see inflation, they can settle debts with less money.

3. In times of recession, governments seek to boost economic growth by making more money available in the market.

Chapter 6: Economy Going Into Recession

What Does It Mean?

In the past couple of times, people have had the opportunity to hear lots about the recession. But, most the majority of people don't know much about it, aside from the fact that it's a kind of economic crisis that is taking place in the world.

What exactly is recession?

The term "recession" refers to an economic contraction (aggregate output, activities and trade over a period of days or more in the market economy). In essence, it's an economic slowdown. But, in addition to the various causes that cause recession, it is necessary for recession to be declared by authorities. The United States, recession is recorded according to the Business Cycle Dating Committee of the National Bureau of Economic Research (NBER). According to NBER it is a major decrease in economic activity lasting longer than a few months. Most prominent researchers, policy makers as well as economists and business use NBER for a exact information about the timing of recession's beginning and its end.

The United Kingdom and the European Union have different definitions of recession. It is defined as having two successive quarters with negative economic growth. Growth in the economy is measured through quarterly quarter-on-quarter estimates in actual GDP (gross domestic product).

What is the cause of recession?

The reason for recession is usually a the widespread decline in spending which could be caused by external trade shocks or financial crisis. other reasons such as:

* Inflation is defined as the percentage at which the average price of certain goods increases, and at the same time the loss of purchasing power. In the event of this central banks attempt to stop the rise in inflation by attempting to reduce the price increase to a the minimum. However, this doesn't always succeed. Inflation may be due to the country's debt, the high cost of energy, and rising production costs. This causes the increase of unemployment rates; businesses eliminate

workers to reduce costs, which could lead to recession.

A high interest rate can limit the liquidity of money that can be used to invest. Investments are not made, which means there is there is no business, and this results in a decrease in economic activity.

* Decreased consumer confidence-everything depends on consumers. If they're not confident in the economy, or if they aren't convinced that certain markets will perform well then they will not invest. Consumer confidence is a matter of perception and can affect the economic performance.

* Reduced real wages or real wages is a phrase that refers to the workers' wages adjusted to inflation. When real wages begin to decline is a sign that workers' wages aren't keeping pace with rate of inflation. The workers earn similar amounts of income, however as inflation increases their purchasing power has decreased.

Types and forms of recession

The economists employ shapes to explain different kinds of recessions. It's an informal way to help economists monitor and categorize the effects of recessions and subsequent recovery processes that follow.

Shapes of recession are named after the letters that the approximate shape of that economic data is drawn graphs in the course of recession and recovery. Recession shapes vary:

This kind of recession is characterized by the abrupt, yet short, time of economic decline with a trough clear. The majority of recessions are v-shaped. This recession can be seen in one of them. Recession that occurred in 1953, which was United States.

* U-shape lasts longer than a v-shaped recession and its trough hasn't been clearly established. In this type of recession the GDP declines in a few quarters, but shows only modest growth following. The best illustration of this type of recession is the US 1973-75 recession.

* W-shape is also known as Double dip recession. This kind of recession is characterized by a dip into recession, regaining from it only to fall back into recession. The recession that began in the

early 1990s within the United States is the example of a w-shaped recession.

* L-shape-is the worst type of recession. it is triggered when the economy enters recession and fails to get back to growth that is trending. This typically lasts for a lengthy duration, and the best example of an L-shaped recession is the recession seen in Japan in the year 1990.

What are the consequences of recession?

Recession is a traumatic event with many negative effects. It causes a rise in unemployment which has a significant impact on the household income. In times of recession, the rate of birth declines because married couples decide not to have children due to financial difficulties.

The recession is when the number of divorces rises also. Money issues are the main reason to divorce and the numbers will only increase during the recession and financial crisis.

Recession can have a negative effect on the young too. They lead to an increase in malnutrition, which can also lead to academic-underachievement. Furthermore, because of unemployment or low wages parents often aren't capable of sending their children to university.

Other effects of the recession are:

* Falling stocks-simultaneously, with the decrease of companies'revenue, the stocks start falling. Their dividends could plummet or even disappear completely. Shareholders aren't satisfied with the business of the company and can invest in companies that generate more profit. This could lead to an even greater decrease in stocks of the company.

If customers have debts to a specific firm, their payment schedules aren't consistent during the recession, or are lower than they are in the past or, in some cases, they do not make any payments in full. Because of the lower revenue and lower profits, businesses have to pay for their own bills and debts at a lower rate which affects the company's ability to meet its obligations.

Employees are laid off due to reduced revenue, businesses have to end agreements with employees. This means that more work will be completed by fewer employees. This can lead to an increase in employees'productivity, but at the same time, morale of the workers decreases, as they are still paid the same amount of money for a larger amount of work. Workers are forced to defend their rights by striking, since their wages are not consistent or even non-existent.

• A decrease in the quality of goods or services as well as a decrease in revenues sometimes force companies to compromise high-quality products or services to make products at a cheaper prices. The consumers are aware of the lower quality which impacts the revenue of companies more. Businesses have a variety of ways to cutting down on quality, such as airlines cut standards for maintenance or add more seats on planes. Food companies provide smaller packs of their products at the same cost.

Companies with lower consumer access have less money to spend on marketing and advertising and this reduces the accessibility of consumers for the item. When fewer customers purchase goods which are less popular, less money is made for the business which increases their vulnerability in the economy.

Can we prevent recession?

There isn't any specific method to stop recession. But, as per economic experts, government officials and monetary authorities are able to adopt policies whose goal is to prevent recessions. For instance:

Cut interest rates - this would increase general demand. A lower interest rate would reduce mortgage interest payments, which could allow consumers to earn more within the household.

In order to prevent the repossession of homes as foreclosures on homes can result in financial losses to banks, it is advised by experts in economics to stop mortgage rates from rising in order to avoid repossessing someone's house.

Taxes are cut - this is done to boost disposable income for consumers. But, this could increase the debt burden of a country because it has to take out loans to pay for the cash shortage, such as, Greece.

* Higher inflation target - this is a reference to a choice to focus on growth rather than inflation.

Chapter 7: Assumptions And Economic

Assumptions

You're now aware of the various aspects in Economics. Maybe it's time to take a examine some of the flaws. This chapter examines some assumptions . The next chapter will examine critiques.

Economics is constantly condemned for its dependence on unobservable, unreasonable or inexplicably based assumptions. Many people respond to this criticism by arguing that the unreliable assumptions in economics stem from abstraction of unimportant details and abstraction is essential to comprehend the complex real world. Therefore, far from being unrealistic assumptions that diminish the value of economics as an epistemic discipline These assumptions are necessary to understand economics. In this way, we can call the abstractionist defense after deconstructing abstraction, unrealistic assumptions and similar notions certain studies have demonstrated that this defense of abstraction cannot effectively counter the arguments of the people who critique economics because of its untruthful assumptions.

Economics is constantly criticised for its reliance on faulty assumptions. Many people respond to this criticism by arguing that the faulty assumptions in economics stem from abstraction from irrelevant details and abstraction is required to comprehend the complex real world. Thus, far from being untrue assumptions that diminish the epistemic value of economics, these assumptions are crucial to economic understanding. This is what I call the line of argument the Abstractionist Defense'. After deconstructing abstraction, unrealistic assumptions and similar notions I demonstrate how the Abstractionist Defence does not successfully counter the arguments of those who attack economics because of its unreliable assumptions.

Abstract: Journal of Economic Methodology Volume 3 Number 2 December 1996

The pitfalls of abstraction and untrue assumptions in economics by Steven Rappaport

Certain assumptions to be considered:

The macroeconomic analysis of Keynesian economics is based on three main assumptions: rigid prices, effective demand and the determinants of savings-investment. First rigid or inflexible prices hinder certain markets from reaching equilibrium in the short term. The second reason is that spending on consumption is dependent on income and not equilibrium or full employment income. Furthermore, significant variables affecting savings and investment include expectations, income, and other factors that go beyond that of the rate at which interest is charged. These three assumptions suggest that the economy is able to achieve an equilibrium for the short term in less than full-employment output.

Classical economics, especially as directed toward macroeconomics, relies on three key assumptions--flexible prices, Say's law, and saving-investment equality. Flexible prices guarantee that markets are able to adjust to equilibrium and eradicate surpluses and shortages. Say's law says that supply generates its own demand. This ensures that enough revenue is generated through production to buy the resultant production. The savings-investment equalization ensures that any money lost from savings into consumption is replaced with an equal quantity of savings. While it is doubtful of its realism the three assumptions implied that the economy will be fully employed.

The central assumption of economics is that humans are rational and efficient in maximizing their personal satisfactions. The latter, however suggests that humans respond to incentives.

Why are wages so rigid? This question is definitely an important one in the field of economics. It is crucial because it's in conflict with two commonly cited beliefs in economics: individuals can be rational, selfish maximizers in the sense the fact that (labour) market prices are highly competitive. Particularly in times of recession when labour is in oversupply, wages should be cut to free the labour market. But, wage reductions are extremely rare and don't even occur in non-regulated unionised markets. [5]

In what other areas of Economics do you find assumptions? If there is a 'model' or a theory, there are assumptions. Consider the model of International Trade - and the assumptions we must make when we look at absolute and comparative advantages. What is the assumption under the conditions of perfect concurrence...

Buddhist Views of Economic Concepts

The fundamental model of economic activity is usually portrayed in textbooks about economics such as that unlimited desires are controlled by scarcity shortage requires choices; choosing comes with some cost of opportunity (i.e. the choice of one option over the other) and the ultimate objective is to achieve the highest level of satisfaction. The core concepts that are present throughout this model -- desire consumption, choice, as well as satisfaction define the essential activities of life from an economic point of view. These concepts are founded on certain assumptions about the human condition. However, the assumptions that modern economists make regarding human nature can be confusing.

Buddhism is, contrary to popular belief provides a consistent and clear picture of human nature. A perspective that encompasses the importance of ethics as well as the two-fold character of desire. Let's now examine some of the economic concepts that are that are based on Buddhist philosophy.

Comments?

Value

In the last chapter, we looked at the two types of desires, chanda and Tanha. Because there are two types of desire so it is obvious that there are two types of value, that we may refer to as true value and artificial value. Value is accomplished through the process of chanda. That is to say the true value of a product can be measured by its capacity to fulfill the requirements for health and well-being. Contrarily artificial value is created through tanha, which is the capacity of a commodity to satisfy the need to feel pleasure.

To evaluate the worth of an object it is necessary to determine what kind of desirethe tanha or the chandathat is what defines the object. The most fashionable clothes, jewelry, high-end cars, and other status symbols are a great source of value that is artificial due to their desire to be pampered and their vanity. Luxury cars may fulfill similar purposes as a less expensive car however, it is priced at a higher cost mainly due to their artificial significance. A lot of the things we take as normal in modern day consumer culture -- such as the media, games and the myriad of junk food that are availablewere created to satisfy tanha. They serve no reason whatsoever and can be harmful to your health. In the majority of cases advertising is a way to promote this artificial value. Advertisers entice us to buy through the projection of appealing images onto the items they sell. They make us believe, for instance that anyone who has the money to buy a luxury vehicle will be different from the rest and belong to the elite, or when we drink a certain type of soft drink, we'll have a lot of friends and will be content.

The real significance of an item can be usually diminished by the artificial value of an object. The desire for conceit and cravings, as well as the desire to be attractive and fashionable are a hindrance to any assessment of the real value of items. For example consider the real significance or motives behind eating food or dressing?

Comments?

Consumption

The issue of consumption is similar to the question of value. We need to distinguish what type of desire we are meant to satisfy Is it to satisfy the need for objects that are truly valuable, or is it to enjoy the pleasures offered by fake value? Consumption is believed to be one of the purposes of economic activities. But, the economic theory and Buddhism differ in their definition of consumption.

Consumption is the relief or fulfillment of desire and satisfaction of desire, which is widely accepted. The modern economics definition of consumption is basically the utilization of products and services to satisfy demands. Buddhism however distinguishes between two types of consumption that could be referred to as "right" consumption or "wrong" consumer. Right consumption refers to the use of goods and services that satisfy the desire for wellbeing. It is a consumption that has the intention of achieving a goal or. Unsane consumption results from tanha, which is the use of products and services in order to satisfy the desire to feel pleasant feelings or to satisfy ego.

Although the Buddhist view is based on an expansive view of the flow of causes and consequences, the economics-specific thinking recognizes only a portion of that stream. Demand results in consumption, which ultimately results in satisfaction. For many economists, that's the end of the story, there's no need to consider the next step. According to this perspective the term "consumption" can mean any type, so long as it leads to satisfaction. It is not a factor in the degree to which well-being will be negatively affected by the consumption.

Consumption can satisfy your sexual desires But its real goal is to promote well-being. Our body, for instance, is dependent on food to nourish itself. Food consumption is essential for a healthy lifestyle. However, for the majority of people eating food is an opportunity to enjoy satisfaction. When eating food, you experience an exquisite taste and a pleasant taste, then one is said to have satisfied one's cravings. The economists often think in this manner, claiming that satisfaction is the consequence of consumption. However, the real question is: what is the real purpose behind eating food? Is it to satisfy desires or the achievement of health?

According to the Buddhist belief that consumption is a way to enhance wellbeing, it is considered to be productive. In contrast it is not a result of consumption in satisfaction and satisfaction then it is not successful. When it comes to the most extreme, drinking tanha can destroy its main purpose that is to improve wellbeing. Indulging in a desire without regard for the consequences can lead to negative effects and loss of actual well-being. Additionally, the obsession with consumption of our culture creates an unnatural discontent. It's odd that economics, which is the science of satisfaction and well-being acknowledges, and even praises the type of consumption that hinders the achievement of its own goals.

In contrast, a healthy consumption will always improve wellbeing and provides a foundation to further develop human potentialities. This is a vital aspect that is often ignored by economists. Chanda-based consumption goes beyond satisfying one's cravings and improves one's well-being and spiritual growth. This is true also globally. If all economic activity was directed by chanda outcome would be more than just a flourishing economy and material growth -these actions would be beneficial to the overall development of humanity and allow humanity to live more noble lives and live an older-style of happiness.

Comments?

Moderation

The very essence in Buddhism is the concept of moderateness. If the purpose in economic endeavor is believed as satisfying desires, the economic process is not defined and is devoid of definition. The desires can be endless. In the Buddhist method economic activity should be controlled with the condition that it's directed towards the pursuit of happiness instead of seeking the "maximum satisfaction" that is the goal of conventional economic thought. Being well-being is an objective concept that is a means of controlling economic activities. There is no longer a struggle with each other to satisfy our endless needs. Instead, our efforts are focused on the pursuit of health and well-being. If the economic activity is directed in this manner it has clear goals and the activities of the business are monitored. Balance or equilibrium is reached. There isn't any excess, nor is there any excessive consumption or overproduction. In the traditional economic model that is controlled by unlimited desires, they is controlled by the scarcity however, under the Buddhist model, they are controlled through a sense of appreciation for moderateness and the goal of wellbeing. The resultant balance naturally reduces the negative consequences of economic activity that is not controlled.

Buddhist Monks and Nuns typically meditate on moderation prior to every meal, reciting the following reflection:

"Wisely considering, we consume alms-giving food, but not for enjoyment, nor for indulgence or the pleasure of tasting however, it is for the sake of maintaining the body, for the continuation of our existence, for the end of suffering in order to live the highest existence. By eating this way can help us overcome uncomfortable feelings of hunger and keep new feelings of pain (of eating too much) from coming up. This is how we can live our lives unhindered without guilt and at ease." [M.I.10; Nd. 496]

The aim of moderation does not have to be restricted to monastics. Anytime we consume something such as clothing, food or even paper and electricity, we should contemplate on their real purpose instead of using them in recklessly. Through this process of reflection, we can avoid excessive consumption and thus be able to recognize "the appropriate amount," the "middle method."

It is also possible to view consumption as a means of achieving achieve a goal, which is the growth of the human capacity. As we strive to develop ourselves as a aim, we eat food, not to enjoy the pleasure it brings however, we consume it to gain the mental and physical energy needed to develop our intellectual and spiritual capacities toward a better life.

Comments?

Non-consumption

With no spiritual aspect Modern economic thought encourages excessive consumption. It is awe-inspiring to those who consume the most -at least three, four or more times per day. If a person were to take a snack every day for ten days it would be a great thing. However the person who practices Buddhist economics believes that a lack of consumption can be a contributing factor to wellbeing. Although monks only eat one meal a day they seek to achieve a level of wellbeing that is dependent on a small amount of.

On days of observance, some Buddhist laypeople are also advised to avoid eating food after noon and, by doing so can contribute to their personal wellbeing. Refraining from eating at night permits them to engage in meditation and contemplation of the Buddha's instructions. The body is relaxed and the mind is calm when the stomach isn't full. Therefore, Buddhism acknowledges that certain demands can be fulfilled by avoiding consumption, a notion that traditional economic thought is difficult to comprehend. Eating less food can play an important role in satisfying our non-material, spiritual requirements.

It's not as if just eating one daily meal is the ultimate goal but, it is. Much like consumption, non-consumption is merely a means to attain a goal, but not a final goal. If abstinence didn't lead to a healthy lifestyle then it's pointless it's just a method to treat ourselves badly. The issue isn't whether or not however, it is whether or not our choices result in self-development.

Comments?

Over consumption

The modern world encourages excessive consumption. In the constant struggle to satisfy their cravings through consumption numerous people harm their health and injure others. Alcohol consumption, for example can satisfy a desire however, it can lead to poor health, unhappy families and even fatal accidents. People who consume food for pleasure tend to overeat and become sick. Some people do not pay attention at all about food's nutritional value and spend their money on food that isn't worth it. Many people are deficient in particular minerals and vitamins despite eating a large meal every day. (Incredibly malnutrition cases have been identified.) In addition to doing them nothing, their eating habits causes others to starve themselves.

We cannot conclude that something is valuable solely because it gives enjoyment and happiness. If one seeks satisfaction in objects that don't enhance your life quality, then the outcome is often the demise of real welfare which can lead to delusion, drinking, and a decline in health and well-being.

The most well-known economic principle is that the primary worth of goods is their capacity to provide satisfaction to the customer. This is why we can point to the above examples where high consumption and intense satisfaction can have positive and negative effects. The Buddhist view is that the worth of both goods and services lies in their capacity to give consumers a feeling of satisfaction improving the quality of their life. This is a crucial clause. Every definition, regardless of services, goods, or social and personal wealth, have to be changed in this manner.

Comments?

Contentment

Although it is not a strictly economic issue, I would like to make some thoughts regarding contentment. It is a virtue that is often misunderstood when it comes to satisfaction and consumption it is a topic that merits an examination.

The primary goal of economics is a sustainable economy in which each demand and desire is fulfilled and continuously replenished in an ever-growing cycle. The whole system is fuelled by the tanha. From a Buddhist viewpoint, this constant pursuit of satisfying desires is in itself a type of suffering. Buddhism advocates the end of this kind of craving or happiness as a more shrewd goal.

Traditional economists may argue that, if there was no desire, the entire economy would come to a slow halt. But, this argument is due to misconceptions about how contentment is defined. Many people misunderstand the concept of contentment since they do not differentiate between two distinct types of desire, tanha as well as chanda. We mix them up and, in promoting the concept of contentment, we dismiss both. A person who is content can be viewed as someone who is not looking for anything. Here lies our mistake.

Evidently, those who are content have less needs than people who are unhappy. But, a proper definition of what is considered to be content must be defined by the condition that it is merely the absence of any artificial desire which is known as tanha. Chanda, the need for real happiness, is still. The way to be truly content is eliminating the desire to create pleasure, and actively encouraging and facilitating the desire for a more satisfying life.

The two steps of reducing tanha and encouraging chanda mutually beneficial. When we feel content with material objects this means we can save energy and time that would otherwise be spent searching for objects that tanha can provide. The energy and time saved can be put to use in the improvement of wellbeing that is the aim of the chanda. When it comes to creating skilled conditions, however, satisfaction is not a good quality. Skilful conditions can only be achieved through hard work. Being too content with regard to chanda is a quick way to turn into apathy and complacency. In this regard the Buddha said that his personal journey to attaining enlightenment was mostly the result of two things that were unending effort and insatiableness with the most skillful circumstances. [D.III.214; A.I.50; Dhs. 8, 234]

Comments?

Work

Buddhist traditional economics and Buddhist differ in their understanding about the importance of work. Contemporary Western economics is founded on the notion the work we do is one is required of us to earn cash for consumption. It is during times that we're not working or enjoying "leisure time" when we are able to feel content and happy. The concepts of satisfaction and work are thought as distinct and in general different concepts.

Buddhism however recognizes that work can be satisfying or not in the case of which type of desires are driving it. If the work is motivated by a desire to be well There is satisfaction in the immediate and immediate outcomes of the work. In contrast, if work is motivated by desire for pleasure, the results directly derived from the work are not as significant. If this is the case it is an inevitable necessity to get the object you want. The distinction between these two perspectives is the one that determines whether or how work will directly affect your wellbeing. In the first working can be a enjoyable activity, but in the second case, it's an essential chore.

To illustrate these two distinct views, let's consider two researchers. Both are researching ways to control pests naturally to use in agriculture. The first researcher Dr. Smith, desires the direct benefits of his work in terms of knowledge and practical application. He is extremely proud of his research. The discoveries and advancements made by him give him satisfaction.

The other, The third one. Jones, only works for promotions and money. Knowledge and the application of it, the results directly derived from his work, aren't the only thing he wants but are just an instrument through which he will eventually gain an income and a positions. He. Jones doesn't enjoy his job, but he is doing it because he believes that it is his duty to.

Working to satisfy the need for health and well-being may bring satisfaction because it's recognized for the sake of it. The achievement and the progress made in the process can result in an increasing sense of satisfaction at each stage of the process's progress. In Buddhist terms it is referred to as working using the chanda. In contrast, working from a desire for pleasure is known as working with the tanha. People who work with tanha are driven with the need to eat. Since it is difficult to consume while working simultaneously working, the task itself provides only a little pleasure or satisfaction. It is also important to point out that working in this instance hinders satisfaction and, as such, is seen as obstruction to it. When work is viewed as a barrier to consumption, it could become unaffordable. In countries that are developing, this can be evident in the amount of corruption and hire-purchase debt in which consumers are unable to tolerate the time lag between working and eating the things they want.

In the modern industrial economy there are many jobs that don't offer satisfaction or make it extremely challenging, due to their nature. The work environment in factories can be boring monotonous, boring, and even hazardous for health. They cause frustration, boredom and depression. All of these affect productivity negatively. Even in mundane or minor tasks, there's an important distinction between working with tanha versus working using chanda. even in the most mundane of jobs, it is difficult to generate feelings of pride in the result of their efforts or a desire to do the task properly or feel a sense of satisfaction in one's accomplishments can ease the monotony, and may even bring satisfaction in the process even though the task isn't always enjoyable it is a feeling that you're developing skills like endurance and has the ability to generate an enthusiasm for the task.

As we've observed that the purpose of tanha rests in the pursuit and acquiring objects that provide pleasure. Although this may require actions, the goal of tanha isn't directly connected in a causal manner to the actions taken. Let's consider two different tasks and analyze the causes and effects that are involved: (1) Mr. Smith cleans the streets and is paid $500 per monthly; (2) When Little Suzie is finished with the book she's going through, Daddy will take her to the movie.

At first impression that sweeping the street is the reason for Mr. Smith receiving his wage and earning his wage. That is, cleaning the streets is the reason and the money is the consequence. In reality, however this is an incorrect conclusion. In fact, one could suggest that the action of sweeping the streets is the main reason behind the street to be cleaned; the cleanliness of the streets is a requirement that the Mr. Smith receiving his wage in accordance with an agreement between the employer and the employee.

Each action produces consequences that are the natural result. The result of sweeping the streets is an uncluttered street. In the contract between the employer as well as employee clause is in addition to the natural outcome which means that cleaning the street can bring the possibility of a cash payment. This is a man-made or artificial law. But, money isn't the result of simply cleaning the streets: certain people might sweep the streets but receive no compensation for doing it, whereas others earn a salary and do not have to clean streets. It is a socially constructed or artificially created condition. A variety of social problems today stem from confusion about the natural outcomes of human actions and the requirements that accompany them. Many people begin to believe that a cash payment is actually the result of sweeping the streets, or, as an alternative instance, that a decent salary, not medical knowledge is the result of learning about medicine.

For Little Suzie It could appear that the completion of the book is what caused it and that going to the films along with Dad is the consequence. However, in reality, reading the book is just an agreement upon which going to cinema is founded. The main benefit of the book is learning.

Extending these examples In the event that Mr. Smith's job is controlled exclusively by tanha the he desires is 500 dollars, and not cleanliness of the streets. In reality the opposite is true. He doesn't wish to clean the streets even once, but as it's a requirement for earning his wages that the requirement is that he has to. For Little Suzie If her primary goal is to go to the cinema (not to read a book) and read, then reading won't give her no pleasure She only reads as a requirement for seeing a movie.

If people are solely working using tanha for their work the real motivation is to consume, not take taking action. Their actions , for example reading, sweeping, and sweepingare considered to be a way of obtaining the items of their desire, such as pay and trips to the cinema. When they are working with chanda on the other the other hand Mr. Smith takes pride in (i.e. wants) the cleanliness of the streets, and little Suzie is looking for the information contained within the text. Chanda is a method of expressing their desire. is to take action and the results that come from this action. Cleanliness is the result of cleaning the streets and understanding is the consequence of studying the book. Once the task is complete the outcome naturally and in a timely manner, appears. If Mr. Smith sweeps the street there is a clean street every time the sweeper is in. When Little Suzie is reading an article, she learns when she is reading the book. When you work with chanda, it is in and of its own realization of the goal.

The purpose of chanda is the action, and the result that is derived from it. If their actions are influenced by the chanda the Mrs. Smith applies himself to cleaning the streets regardless of the amount he earns each month and little Suzie is able to read her book without Daddy needing to pledge to take her to the movie. (In the real world it is true that most people are employed for income, which is necessary however, we also have the option to be proud of our work and work hard to perform it with excellence by chanda or do it just to earn a wage. So, in actual situations, individuals are motivated through different amounts of both tanha and the chanda.)

As we've observed the actions motivated by chanda as well as actions motivated by tanha result in completely different outcomes in terms of both ethics and objectively. If we are motivated by tanha , and just trying to get some unrelated item or method to consume, we could be enticed to obtain the desired object by other methods that require lesser effort. If we are able to achieve the goal without any effort whatsoever, that's even better. If it is essential to accomplish the goal but we'll just do it slowly and with a minimal degree of effort.

The ultimate result is criminality. When Mr. Smith wants money but doesn't have the motivation (chanda) for work, he might find the work infuriating and decide to steal. If Little Suzie would like to go to the cinema, but she can't read the novel, she might take money from her mother and then go to the cinema by herself.

With just tanha for their wages, but no chanda to complete their job, the people just go through the motions of their jobs and do what they can to survive. This results in apathy, lazyness, and poor work. It's a case of laziness, obliviousness and poor craftsmanship. Smith simply goes through his routine of sweeping the streets day in and day until payday arrives when Little Suzie begins reading the book just to allow Daddy be aware that she's completed it. She isn't absorbed by anything she's read. Or she might lie and claim that she's completed the book, but actually she hasn't.

When dishonesty and sloppy behavior that are of this kind occur within the workplace, further screenings should be implemented to keep an eye on the activities. These steps address the signs but not the root cause which only increases the difficulty of the situation. For instance, it could be necessary to assign the supervision of Mr. Smith's work and verify his hours. Or Little Suzie's brother might need to check whether she's actually studying the book. This goes for employers and employees as well. tribunals for workers must be set up to stop employers who are irresponsible or greedy from squeezing their employees and requiring them to endure inhumane conditions or with unfair pay. If tanha is the driving force, both employers and workers are stuck in a race of one-upmanship, both sides trying to gain as much as they can with the lowest cost.

Tanha is elevated to a large extent due to social forces. For instance, if people in charge of the equipment of production are driven by the desire to become wealthy with as little expense as they can, it's highly unlikely that the employees will enjoy a great deal of chanda. They are more inclined to follow in the footsteps of their bosses and try to achieve as much as they can with the least effort possible. This is evident in the contemporary workplace. It appears, in addition, that the more wealthy an area becomes, the more of this behavior develops -the more we have and the more we want. This is due to the rapid growth of tanha that is unchecked and the absence of a alternatives that are viable. In the meantime, the ideals of inner peace and contentment of mind appear to be largely lost in our modern world.

In rare instances we do hear of employees and employers working together chanda. This is in situations where the company is accountable competent and compassionate in order to win the trust and love of employees who , in turn, are well-organized, efficient and dedicated to their job. There have been instances that employers have been so compassionate for their employees that, when their business fell apart and were close to bankruptcy, their employees kindly offered sacrifices and did everything they could to make the business profitable once again. Instead of demanding the payment of compensation they were prepared to cut pay.

Comments?

Production and Non-production

The term "production" is not accurate. It is a common misconception that by producing, the creation of new objects is happening but in reality it's simply changes in the state that are affected. A particular substance or type of energy is transformed into another. The conversions result in the formation of a new state by the destruction of the existing one. Therefore, production is always followed by destruction. In certain situations, the destruction is considered acceptable, but in other cases it isn't. Production can only be justified as long as the benefit of the product produced is greater than the item that is destroyed. In some instances, it might be more beneficial to avoid production. This is usually the case in industries whose products serve destruction. In factories for weapons For instance it is the preferred option. In the case of industries that require depletion of the natural resource as well as the degradation of the environment in some cases, non-production can be the most effective option. When choosing, it is important to discern between production that has positive outcomes and production that has negative outcomes; production that improves our well-being, and one that destroys it.

In this context, non-production is a viable economic option. Someone who makes very minimal materially could however consume less of the resources of the world and live a life which is beneficial to the people around him. A person like this is of higher value than one who systematically consumes huge amounts of the world's natural resources while making goods that are harmful to the society. Modern economics can't discern this distinction; it would be lauding those who produce as well as consumes (that is destroys) massive quantities more than someone who creates and consumes (destroys) very little.

In the economy of the industrial age, the word "production" has been assigned a limited meaning. It's thought to apply to things that are able to be bought and sold. A bull fight, in which people pay to watch the slaughter of bulls, can be viewed as being a source of income however children caring for an older person in the street isn't. comedians who perform on stage, calming his audience and offering them an enjoyable time, is considered to be economically productive due to the fact that money moves around, whereas an office worker who has an extremely positive attitude isn't considered to have made anything through his jovial attitude towards those who are around them. Also, there is no account of the economic cost of loud speech and aggressive actions that create stress within the workplace which means that the people who are affected must find a method to relieve it using entertainment options, such as attending a comedy show.

Comments?

Cooperation and Competition

Modern economics is founded on the notion that it is the human nature to be competitive. Buddhism in contrast acknowledges that humans have the capacity to be competitive and collaboration.

The natural way to win is when people are seeking to satisfy the need for pleasure -- and when they are driven by tanhapeople will be competitive. In these instances, they are determined to achieve as much as they can for themselves and do not feel any satisfaction or sense of fulfillment. If they are able to obtain the object they want without sharing it with others then so be it. It is inevitable that competition will be fierce as is the nature of the mind that is influenced by the tanha.

This competitive urge could be used to encourage collaboration. It could be possible to bring together the members of a specific group by encouraging them to be competitive with another group. For instance, managers from corporations often rally their employees to defeat their rivals. However, this type of cooperation is based solely on competition. Buddhism refers to this as "artificial collaboration."

The true spirit of cooperation comes from the desire for wellbeing -by the chanda. Human development requires us to recognize how chanda and tanha can motivate us and switch our attention away towards cooperation instead of competition to resolve the issues that face the world and attain a greater goal.

Comments?

Choice

"Whether an individual's desire is truly a need or just a wishful thought or a strange desire is not relevant to economics. Also, it is not the responsibility of economics to decide if the desires of a person ought to be satisfied,"[2according to the economics literature, however, from an Buddhist standpoint, the choices we make are of paramount significance, and the decisions require a certain understanding of the options that are available. Choice is the result of intention, and is the basis of kamma. It is one of the fundamental teachings of Buddhism. The impact of kamma is not just economics, but also every aspect of our lives as well as our natural and social environment. Economic decisions, also known as choices that are not based on ethical considerations are considered to be bad kamma and they are likely to produce negative outcomes. Economic decisions that are good are made with a clear understanding of the costs at the personal, social and environmental scales, not only in terms of consumption or production. These decisions in the economic realm are known as kamma. When an economic decision is made, kamma gets created, and the process of bringing it to fruition is initiated, whether either way for the individual, society, and for the environment. Therefore, it is crucial to understand the difference in quality between various options and make decisions carefully.

Comments?

Life Views

I'd like to step back and consider economics from a broader view. We've discussed the different economic actions. It is now time to ask what's the goal of these actions? What do we hope to achieve through all this selling and buying production and consumption? We could be asking a bigger question: What exactly is the point of existence?

Everyone has their own opinions about these issues, but the majority of us are unaware of these. Buddhist doctrines emphasize the fact that these views have immense effect on how we live our lives. They also stress that these views have a profound impact on our lives. Pali word for viewpoint is ditthi. It encompasses all kinds of views at a variety of levels - our personal beliefs and opinions and ideologies; beliefs and views of religion and politics embraced by various groups; and the beliefs and views shared by all societies and cultures.

The impact of views extends beyond the realms of mental states and discussions. Similar to ethics, opinions are connected to the stream of causes and the conditions. It is "subjective" mental constructs which in turn affect the events of "objective" real-world reality. On a personal scale your worldview can affect the way that life unfolds. At a national level politics and social norms affect society and affect the everyday life quality.

The Buddha warned that the view of views is likely to be the most dangerous of all mental disorders. Insane views can cause irreparable harm. The violent nature that erupted from the Crusades, Nazism and Communism for instance, three of the most destructive fanatical movements, were all fueled by extremely unskilful opinions. Skilful perspectives however are the most effective of mental states. The Buddha stated: "Monks, I see any other condition that's as much a reason for the development of yet to be arose unskillful conditions, as well as for the development and growth of the unskillful condition that has already been created from a wrong perspective ..." [A.I.30The wrong view [A.I.30]

This raises the question of what philosophy of life lies the basis of the modern economy? Are they skilled or untrained one? In the event of simplifying the issue, let us declare that the purpose of our modern lives is to achieve happiness. This notion is so widespread in our modern society that it's not often thought of, let alone studied or even questioned. The very notion of "progress" -- whether it's social technological, scientific, economic and even political is based on the assumption that the goal of society is to achieve a society that everyone is content. In the United States Declaration of Independence poetically represents this ideal by defending mankind's right to "life liberty, liberty, and happiness."

Although it is certainly a noble idea, the notion to make happiness the aim of life is a fundamental misconception about the reality of living. "Happiness" is nothing more than an unclear and unattainable quality. A large portion of people think that happiness is feelings of pleasure and satisfaction of their wants. For many the concept of happiness is a distant thing, something beyond them as a goal to be pursued and seized. However, happiness is not attainable via a search, it is only possible through making the factors and circumstances that create it. And they are mental and personal growth.

From a Buddhist viewpoint It is commonplace for people to misinterpret tanha, their constant craving for pleasure and pleasure with the search for happiness. This is an unwise idea, since the desire of tanha is never satisfied. If the quest for happiness is the same as the desire to pursue things that tanha is a part of then life itself is a miserable experience. To comprehend the implications of this untrue perspective, just observe the despair and anger of people living in numerous modern cities brimming with endless entertainment and leisure centers. Instead of leading to happiness and wellbeing the search for happiness often results in anxiety and exhaustion within the individual, conflict in the society, and unsustainable consumption of the environment.

Contrastingly with the Buddhist perspective on life is not as than idealistic, and is more practical. The Buddha declared, "There is suffering." [Vin.I.9; S.V.421; Vbh.99This was the initial of his Four Noble Truths, the fundamental tenets of Buddhism. He then described the meaning of suffering: "Birth is suffering; old years are a source of suffering; sickness is suffering and death is suffering. sadness, sorrow, despair and grief are suffering; being separated from those you love is suffering. Receiving what you don't want can be suffering. Not receiving what you want can be a source of suffering. ..."

There is no doubt that these issues are present in life , and are invariably unpleasant, yet the tendency of our culture is to dismiss these realities. Death, specifically is not often thought of or talked about as an inevitable event that is personal to us. The fact is that denying these things, however they will not disappear. That's why the Buddha declared that suffering should be acknowledged. One of the first Noble Truth is the recognition that all things have to be able to pass, and that there is no peace to be found within the world of material things. This is the sort of truth that the Buddha demanded people face -- the very evident and essential realities of life.

2. The Second Noble Truth explains the cause of suffering. The Buddha claimed that the root of all suffering lies in cravings caused by ignorance (that is called Tanha). That is that the reason for pain is not an external problem. It is possible to be asking, "Does craving cause old age? " It isn't the craving that triggers the onset of old age, but it is wanting to live longer, which causes old age to be a source of pain. The aging process is inevitable, but the desire to be a part of it isn't. The Buddha claimed that craving can be eliminated. This brings we to the 3rd Noble Truth which is about the end of suffering. By complete and complete abstention from the desire for pleasure, suffering is eliminated. But how do we achieve this? in the 4th Noble Truth the Buddha tells the way. The Noble

Eightfold Path for the cessation of suffering through the instruction of mind, body, and speech in line with the Buddhist code of Right View, Right Thinking and Right Speech. Action, Right Livelihood Right effort, Right Mindfulness and right concentration.

It is pretty clear in reading the Four Noble Truths that the Buddhist perspective on life is opposed to the perspective that is common in modern society. In contrast to Buddhism affirms "There is suffering,"" contemporary societies state, "There is happiness, and I'm looking for it right today!" Its implications for this shift in perspective are huge. A society that regards the main purpose of life to be an attempt to achieve happiness is naive in pursuing a future vision. Happiness is viewed as something intrinsically missing and needs to be found elsewhere. With this belief comes tension, frustration, impatience and a failure to deal with pain and suffering, as well as the inability to pay attention to the present.

However when we have a perspective of living that acknowledges the reality that we suffer, it is important to pay greater focus on the present in order to spot difficulties when they come up. We work with other people in solving issues, instead of fighting with them to achieve happiness. This view is also reflected in our choices in the realm of economics. Our consumption and production are not geared toward the pursuit of pleasure (tanha) instead towards alleviating the pain (chanda). If this Buddhist idealism were to be adopted on a global or national scale, instead of seeking to satisfy every need our economic systems would endeavor to achieve a state devoid of suffering or a state that is set up for the pleasure of happiness (just like a healthy body is is designed to be happy).

Only by understanding the suffering of others will we be able to appreciate how possible it is to be happy. This is why Buddhism distinguishes between two types of happiness dependent happiness in addition to independent. Dependent happiness is a state of mind that is dependent on an external object. It is any happiness that is dependent on the material world that includes family, wealth, honour and fame. Dependent happiness, based on things that cannot be ours in the ultimate sense, is unstable and unpredictable.

Independent happiness However, independent happiness is the joy that is a result of an inner mind that is trained and achieved a level in inner tranquility. This kind of happiness isn't dependent on external circumstances and is more secure than dependent happiness.

Dependent happiness causes tension and competition when it comes to acquiring tangible items. Any happiness that results from such activities is a contentious type of happiness. However, there's another type of happiness that is not as awe-inspiring as the more independent type however, is more effective over the contentious type. It's a type of kind of happiness that is more charitable focused, geared towards happiness and motivated by goodwill and compassion. As they grow people are able to appreciate this kind of true happiness, an urge to spread joy to people around the world (which in Buddhism is known as metta). In this type of happiness we feel joy over the joy of others the same way that parents feel happy about the joy in their own children. This type of happiness could be described as "harmonious happiness" as opposed to the more contentious type of happiness. It is not dependent on things of the material world and results more by giving rather instead of receiving. While this happiness isn't entirely self-sufficient, it is more able than happiness resulted from selfish purchases.

The best guarantee of happiness is the freedom of enlightenment that is unchangeable. Yet, the ability to train the mind through study and meditation to attain a sense of inner satisfaction is a powerful solution to the discontents of the society that consumes. In the light of calmness within, comes an understanding of one of the greatest ironies in life In our quest for happiness can cause suffering. by understanding suffering, we can find peace.

Chapter 8: Jokes

This chapter is essentially an assortment of jokes about Economics. However ! As your knowledge of Economics expands, you'll appreciate these 'jokes' funny...hopefully. In the midst of each joke is a "comments box" where you can provide a rationale for the meaning of 'economics' that is being used in this comedy ...

It is possible that you will not find these hilarious, but the most important thing is are you aware of how to understand the Economics of the story. To aid, under every comedy (and it's not just one joke - there's others - do an internet search using Google) there is a space that is left for comments:

Three people have been left stranded on a tiny island. One is a physicist another is a circus strongman and the third one is an economist. After several days of living on fruits, they find the cans of canned food items, and are required to decide on how to open the cans. The scientist suggests"here's the tough guy "Why do you not climb up that tree, smash the cans against the rocks and then blow the cans open?"

The strongman responds, "No, that would spill the contents everywhere. I could open the cans using my teeth!"

The economist states "First we have to assume that we have a canned opener."

Comments:

What is the reason astrology was developed? In order to make economy an exact science.

Comments:

An accountant and an economist are walking across a large puddle. They come across one of the frogs jumping over the mud. The economist states: "If you eat the frog, I'll pay $20,000!"

The accountant reviews his budget and determines the best way to eat it, and so he does and then collects the cash.

As they continue to walk through the same puddle, they are about to step into another frog. The accountant tells them: "Now, if you consume this frog, I'll pay you $20,000." After considering the proposal, an economist decides to eat the frog. The receives the money.

They continue. The accountant thinks: "Listen, we both have the same amount of money that we used to have however, we both have eaten Frogs. I can't imagine us being more fortunate." Economic expert "Well it's true however, you didn't consider our factual involvement in trade. only involved in $40,000 worth or trade."

Comments:

An economist is back to visit his former school. He's curious about the latest examination questions, and asks his former professor to demonstrate some. Surprisingly, they're exactly the same as those which he was able to answer just a decade back! If he questions this the professor replies: "the questions are always identical, only the answers are different!"

Comments:

An economist was reported for having a horseshoe placed above the doorframe of his office. When asked about the purpose the man replied "it is a lucky charm that assists me in my forecasts".

"But are you a believer in this superstition?" He was asked.

"Of no!" He declared, "but it works whether you believe in it or not."

Comments:

An economist was walking out of his office when he saw an adorable boy sitting in the street with an animal. The boy shouted at the economics professional "Hey what would it be like for you to purchase the dog you've always wanted."

The man was fascinated by the sales pitch and proceeded to ask the dog "How many dollars do you think you'd like for your dog."

The boy informed him that "Fifty thousands dollars."

"Fifty million dollars!" the man said in shock. "What specific methods does this dog use that can make him earn enough cash to earn five million dollars?" The man asked the boy.

The boy said, "Mister, this dog has never earned a dime in his entire life. In fact, if you count the food he eats, I think you'll lose dollars every year on him."

The economist deemed this to be an ideal opportunity to talk about economics with the boy and elaborated on the necessity of an item to generate more money than it consumed to be equal to the cost of purchase, which would be the possibility of receiving 5 dollars off someone who was looking for a partner. The economist felt he had taught an important knowledge to the young man The economist continued into the distance.

Then, a few days later the economist was escorted to leave his and the little boy was still sitting on the curb with no dog. The man told his friend, "I see you took my advice and you sold the dog for $5."

The boy replied, "No, I got fifty thousand dollars in exchange for him."

The businessman was stunned. "How did you earn fifty million dollars for the dog" He demanded. "It was simple," said the boy. "I exchanged him for twenty five thousand dollars cats."

Comments:

The economic outlook of the government can be summarized in a few words If it's moving and is taxed, it should be taxed. If it continues to move then regulate it. If it ceases to move and it stops, then you can lower it.

Comments:

Anarchism: You have two cows. The cows decide that you don't have the right to use their milk and decide to create their own society.

Anarchism: You have two cows. You steal the bull of your neighbor and you ignore the government.

Anarchism: You own two cows. You keep them and take another. You do not listen to the authorities.

Anarchism: You own two cows. You can either sell your milk at the right price or your neighbours attempt to seize the cows and slaughter you.

Anarchism: You have two cows. The neighbor hits you on your head using a brick. He takes your cows and shoots them in the name of amusement. Later, you find out that he's the infamous Nazi.

ARISTOCRATISM It is when you have two cows. You decide to sell them and buy one huge cow with pedigree.

Artist -- Visual The cows are two. They're stuffed and placed them in glass display cases. In London.

BAHRAINISM The situation is that you have two cows. A high-ranking official takes one and milks it, then sells the milk, and pocket the money. The government says there's only one cow, and there isn't enough milk for the entire population. People riot and shout death at the government, and wave Iranian flags. The parliament, after having thought for over a year, finally decides to hire 10 Bahrainis for milking all cows simultaneously to decrease unemployment.

BRITISH British: You are the owner of two cattle. They're insane. They are impossible to sell in Europe.

BRITISH MAJOR The cows are two. One of them has BSE. A vet is able to give the other person the all-clear. You the vet declares that there's no problem with BSE within your nation.

BUREAUCRACY: There are two cows. The government first regulates the food is allowed to feed the cows, and when you are allowed to milk them. Then , it doesn't pay you for milking them. After that, it shoots one of them, then milks the other and then pours the milk into the drain. After that, you must complete forms to account for the cows that have gone missing.

BUREAUCRACY: You own two cows. To get them registered, you complete the 17 form in three copies, and do not have the enough time to milk them.

BUREAUCRACY EUROPEAN UNION: There are two cows. In the EU, EU has one cow gone, and then milks another, and afterwards, spills its milk.

BUREAUCRACY UNITED States: You own two cows. The government is able to take both. loses one , while moving it to the farm situated in Puerto Rico and forgets to milk the other.

Canadianism: You own two cows. The bank takes them both and shoots one of them, dumps the milk out, and then you shoot yourself.

Capitalism: You own two cows. You sell one and purchase an animal.

Capitalism -- American Two cows are in your barn. You decide to sell one and then purchase the bull. The bull and cow are in love with each other You sell the movie rights Hollywood. You then enter real estate.

Capitalism --- HONG KONG You own two cows. You sell three to your publicly traded firm, using letters credit issued by your brother-in-law at the bank. You then make a debt or equity swap, with an associated general offer in order to get back all four cows and an income tax deduction to keep five cows. The rights to milk of six cows are transferred through an intermediary in the form of a Panamanian intermediary to an Cayman Islands company secretly owned by the majority shareholder who then sells the rights to all seven cows their milk back to the publicly listed company. The annual report indicates that the company has eight cows, and an option to purchase another. In the meantime, you slaughter two cows due to the fact that Feng Shui is harmful.

Centralism Two cows. They are difficult to find within the fields along with 100,000,000 cows.

CONSERVATIVISM: There are two cows. The milk is frozen and you make the cows embalm.

CONSERVATIVISM: There are two cows. They are locked up and charge people to gaze at them.

There are two cows. The government takes them both and provides you with a part from the cow's milk.

The COMMUNISM system has two cows. The government has both cows. Government sells milk at stores owned by the government. The milk is expensive. You are savage.

The COMMUNISM system is that you have two cows. They are both owned by the state and offers you a bit of liquid milk ... at least once.

COMMUNISM: You own two cows. The government takes both of them and provides you with spoiled milk.

The COMMUNISM --- CAMBODIAN Two cows. The government will take each and kills them.

UNION -- CAMBODIAN The two of you have cows. The government sends a teen wearing a red bandana shoot them. He then shoots you.

COMMUNISM CHINESE: You don't have cows. The government establishes an alliance with McDonald's.

Chinese communists There are two cows. You tend to them. The government gets every drop of milk however you're encouraged to take some back (before you do it by someone else).

CHINESE COMMUNISM - MAO Style: You own two pigs. The government begins an appeal to convince you to give them "voluntarily" in order to provide food for the workers of the city. The government announces that people don't require pork pigs in order to produce it. Invoking the right words from your red book You and your friends attempt to make pork using the power of your determination. The local leader of the party reports that you've exceeded your expectations. Your neighbours starve.

COMMUNISM -- CUBAN - CASTRO STYLE: Fidel Castro has two cows. They're F1's. They're which is a cross between and the Cebu cow as well as the Holstein cow. There is only one Cow, "White Udder," is in operation. In the event of her death, she's put in a museum run by Castro, "The Dictator of the Cows" in which "future generations will be able to admire her stunning udders." There isn't a single cow milk since 1985.

Communism Communalism CUBAN The two of you have cows. Fidel informs you that hidden CIA agents are infecting all cattle in your region with a foreign disease which causes death to the cows. You and your family are undernourished. It becomes apparent to you that Fidel isn't sure what he's talking about.

COMMUNISM -The COMMUNISM - CUBAN It's over. You don't have cows. They left for Miami. There is no milk, but you have Fidel.

COMBUNISM "PURE" The situation is that you have two cows. Your neighbors help you take care of the animals, and you are able to share the milk.

COMBUNISM "PURE" The situation is that you have two cows. Your neighbors help you take care of the cows, and you are sharing the milk. Perhaps the local bully gains more, or maybe a couple of neighbors band together to kill you to ensure that there's milk available for all of us.

COMBUNISM -- SOVIET There are two cows. You are responsible for taking care of them, however the government takes the milk. Then, the government takes you to jail.

COMBUNISM -- SOVIET There are two cows. You take them out and discover the number of cows is four. You sip more Vodka. You go through the count again and you realize that you have eleventy six cows. You drink even more Vodka. After some time you realize that eleventy isn't really a number. You run the numbers again and find two cows. You crack open another container of Vodka and attempt to drown out the loss eleventy-four cows.

Democracies: You own two cows. Your neighbors decide who gets the milk.

Democracies: You own two cows. The vote is taken and the cows prevail.

Democracy: You own two cows. They vote 2-1 against you to prohibit all dairy and meat products. You go bankrupt.

Democracy -- American There are two cows. Your neighbors choose a person to determine who gets the milk. They then they blame Japan as border guards beat Mexicans entering the country. There's a lot of outrage for about a week and then return to sports that are telecast and there is no violence.

DEMOCRACY -American (a republic) Two cows. The government exercise those powers granted through the populace which are the sovereigns. The majority is not in control because the citizens along with their representative (elected appointed, appointed, and employed) are governed by a variety of checks and balances, such as the Constitution and the Bill of Rights, the three co-equal branches in the government as well as the state republics of 50 states (see, e.g., Article IV Section 4.). Also, what is done by the federal government with cows as well as with the milk of the cows will depend on the interactions between people as well as these checks and balances described earlier.

DEMOCRACY BRITISH Two cows. You feed them brains of sheep and they get mad. The government isn't doing anything.

DEMOCRACY -REPRESENTATIVE Two cows reside in your home. The neighbors choose a person to inform you who milks which.

DICTATORSHIP: You own two cows. The government draws both cows, and then drafts you.

DUBAISM: You own two cows. You develop a website to their use and then advertise the cows in all magazines. You develop the concept of a Cow City as well as a Milk Town for them. You then sell your cows' milk prior to the time they have been milked. You sell the milk to legitimate and unscrupulous investors who want to resell the milk for a 100percent profit within 2 years. You send Tiger Woods to milk the cows first in order to draw the attention of.

EGYPTIANISM The world has two cows. Both of them are voting for Moooooobarak!

EUROPEAN UNIONISM The EU has two goats. They are fruit. EU declares them fruit, in order to adhere to a unique Belgian tradition to make Cow Jam (jam being required to have at minimum at least 45% fruit).

EUROPEAN UNIONISM There are two cows. The EU has a quota-based program that "limits the emission of gases caused by flatulent cattle." You can sell your carbon allotment, but not the milk.

FASCISM: You own two cows. The government takes them both and employs you to care for them, and then sells you the milk.

FASCISM: You own two cows. You donate your milk to government, and the government then sells it.

FASCISM: You own two cows. One is taken by the government and then presses to put it in the military.

The FEUDALISM is that you have two cows. Your lord eats a little part of your milk.

FRISBEETARIANISM There are two cows. One of them takes off onto the roof, and then gets stuck. It is hoped that the government will provide cow ladders.

IDEA: You own two cows. You marry and you share milk with your partner.

In the world of industrialization, you are the owner of two dairy cows. You cut them up and determine how you can create a milk factory instead.

IRAQISM The British Government has sent 20 cows for an experimental run to assist the village of Basra. Villagers are very thankful for the extra milk , and the health of children is improving each day. The terrorists then abduct the cows and accuses them being the traitors to "the the cause." The terrorists then create authentic statements from the cattle. They then regularly assassinate them all before Al Jazeera television cameras.

The KUWAITIS: When they hear the popularity of cows within the Gulf region, a small group of males who are young Kuwaitis purchase an entire herd. However, they add to so many extras (ski-racks as well as sub-woofers that are 3500 watts Nipple lights, etc.) that the cows are almost crashing in shame and weight. The entire herd is tragically killed in the heap while their owners trying to make donuts at the Towers.

LEBANONISM The Lebanonian government has two cows. They are owned and operated by Syria and the other one is managed by the government.

LIBERALISM There are two cows. Both are sold to the wealthy. The government then tax the wealthy cow and then gives it to the less fortunate.

LIBERALISM The situation is that you have two cows. You sell one and ask the government to provide you with another cow. Then , you give each one to the public.

LIBERTARIANISM Two cows. They are free to do whatever they like.

LIBERTARIANISM is a sham. My cow's behavior is not your concern.

The proletarian cows unify and defeat the cowherds of the bourgeoisie. The democratic democratic cow revolutionary state, with the cow-party as the vanguard is destined to fall apart with time. Marx took a bite of a veggie-burger before he was able to explain how the value of use as well as the exchange value and sign-value of bovine leather.

NAZISM: You own two cows. Government officials take both, and is then able to shoot you.

NEW DEALISM NEW DEALSM: You own two cattle. The government is able to take both, shoot one of them, milks the second and pours the milk into the drain. The government claims there's the huge storage tank that holds all milk is disposed of.

OMANISM: You own three cows. They're well-fed and provide top quality milk to sell on the market. However, your son finds out that the cash he earned from the market could be used to purchase beer. Your plans to expand your business with an entirely new farm with high-tech technology are put on hold for a while.

PACIFISM: There are two cows. They'll stampede you.

Perotism: You have two cows. It isn't permitted to export the milk into Mexico.

PLATONISM: There are two cows. You are looking for two additional dairy cows.

PLATONISM: You've got an image of two perfectly cows. Their milk is like water. Look for two genuine cows that produce milk.

POLITICAL CORRECTNESSIS The person you are in contact with is (the notion that "ownership" is an expression of the phallocentric, warlordly and intolerance past) two different-aged (but not less important to the world) bovines with no gender.

PROTECTION: You have two cows. You cannot purchase a bull from a different country.

QATARISM It's like having two cows. They've been sat there for years and nobody has realized that cows produce milk. When you realize the things that Dubai does, and you become enraged and start milking cattle in the fastest time you can. You realize that no one was interested in milk at all in the first place.

REDISTRIBUTIONISM There are two cows. Every person should have the identical number of cows. The government cut both cows down, the meat off, and then invests more money than the value of the cows providing everyone with a small portion of cow.

SAUDISM: You own two cows. Since milking a cow is a process that involves nibbles, the government has decided to ban cows in public. The only way to milk the cow is to put the cow in one corner of the curtain, and a man taking milk from the cow at the opposite side.

SIMPSONISM: You don't need an animal!

SOCIALISM: You own two cows. The government will take one and then gives it to your neighbor.

SOCIALISM BUREAUCRATIC: You own two cows. The government gets them and put the animals in barns together with all other cows. They are taken care of by chicken farmers who have left. You must look after the chickens which the government confiscated from chicken farmers. The government will give you eggs and milk as much according to the rules you'll need.

SOCIALISM -Pure: You own two cows. The government will take these cows and put the two cows in barns along with all the other cows. You must take charge of all the cows. The government provides all the milk you require.

SOCRATIC METHODISM What number of cattle do I own? Why?

SURREALISM: There are two Giraffes. The government demands that you learn harmonica.

SURREALISM: There are two Aardvarks. They paint one green , and demands that you learn harmonica.

TALIBANISM: There are two cows. The government initially obliges them to wear burkas however, later they shoot them due to the fact that "they are Hindu symbol of religion."

UNITED NATIONISM: You have two cows. France opposes milking them. It is the United States and Britain veto the cows from milking you. New Zealand abstains.

YEMENISM: Once you had one cow. Then it was kidnapped.

Comments:

How many economists do you need to replace a lightbulb?

* None. If it really required change the marketplace forces could have made it take place.

* None. If the government were to let it be the country would be screwed into.

* None. The invisible hand is the one who does it.

* Two. One is to make the assumption of a ladder and another to switch the bulb.

* Eight. One to modify it, and seven to keep all other things constant.

* One person to draft your proposal. economist for running the model one for each

119

MS or PhD student to compose their dissertations and theses Two more are required to draft the article for publication (senior authorship is not given) Four to read it, and at a minimum at least four to improve the model and duplicate the results.

Comments:

A woman took a stroll through her area and saw a little puppy in a boy's. "Would you like to have a puppy?" said the child. "They aren't quite ready for new homes yet, but they'll be within a couple of weeks!"

"Oh They're adorable!" the woman said. "What kind of dog are they?" "These economics are the dogs," answered the young man.

"O.K. I'll let my husband know." She went back to her home and informed her husband. He was extremely fascinated by the puppies.

After a week when he was walking by, he saw the boy. The puppies were extremely lively. "Hey, Mister. Do you want to have a puppy?" asked the boy. "I believe that my wife talked about this last week with you," said the man. "What kind of dog are they?"

"Oh. These are decision analysts." said the boy with pride. "I I thought you had claimed the other week they are economists,"" said the guy.

"Well it is true," replied the boy. "But the eyes are wide."Comments:

Chapter 9: Implication And Scope Of

Economics

What is the term "economics?

The word that we use today "Economics" is derived from the Greek word "Oikonomos" which means "economy"

Stewards. The two components of the word "Oikos" house, and "nomos" an administrator summarize

What is economics all about? How can we run our home and what kind of stewardship could we give towards our loved ones, the nation, and to our children?

The economic element to nearly every topic we would like to discuss including employment, education transport, housing defense, etc. Economics is a complete understanding of how society operates. As so, it's hard to define. The famous classic economics expert Alfred Marshal defined economics as the "Study of man's normal daily life".

It is, however, an extremely vague definition. The reason is that any definition should be based on the consideration of the principle that drives economics, which is the concept of the concept of scarcity. The famous American economics professor Paul Samuelson thus defined it as: "The study of how society and individuals decide to use limited resources that be used in different ways to create various commodities and disperse them to consumers, today or in the near future, among diverse groups of people and society.

It is true that everything is scarce, not only diamonds and oil but also water and bread. The term "scarcity" in economics refers to the fact that all resources are scarce, as in that they are not enough to meet all the needs of the population enough to satisfy everyone's needs.

Therefore, we have a limited amount of resources that are available both in developed countries as well as in the poorer countries. The role of an economist is to analyze the possibilities that are available to make making use for these sources. This is another aspect of economics, the focus is on choices.

Another factor is the people themselves. They don't just want more food or clothing; they're looking for particular kinds of food items, certain types of clothing, and so on. We are talking about want;

"A materialistic desire to purchase something or an activity. Human desires are endless.

We now have the three essential ingredients of our definition: People (human desires) (human desires), Scarcity, and the option. For our purposes, we can define economics as:

"The social science concerns the distribution of scarce resources in order to supply products and services that meet the demands and needs of consumers"

The Scope of Economics?

Economic studies starts by understanding our "wants". We are forced to reduce our consumption. We consider the many options and choose the variety of goods that provides the greatest return on our resources. Modern economists employ this concept as a basis for defining the general scope of their research.

Although economics is tightly linked to social sciences such as sociology, ethics, political science as well as psychology and anthropology it differs from them by its focus on a specific aspect of human behavior that is the choice between options to achieve the highest satisfaction from limited resources.

In reality the economist restricts the scope of study by identifying four essential characteristics of human beings and analyzing the consequences when they are in a group like they normally are. The first is that the ends of human beings have no any limit. Furthermore, the goals are of different importance. Thirdly, the tools to achieve those ends such as human energy and time as well as material resources are limited. Fourth, the resources can be employed in various ways. That is they are able to produce various items.

Each of these characteristics in and of itself is relevant to an economist. When all of the four aspects are found to be in sync, will an economic issue arise.

Resources: The components which are compiled by economists and are referred to as economic good i.e. products that are scarce proportion to the demand for them.

Economic Goods

All the things that people desire are put together by economists. They call them economically valuable goods i.e. items that are scarce in comparison with the amount of demand that is for these items.

Free Goods

They are items that people are able to have as much of they would like, e.g. air.

2. The METHODOLOGY ECONOMICS and its fundamental concept

Economics is an evolving discipline that studies evidence, making theories, testing them, and achieving sometimes a shaky agreement on how the economy functions. This is known as the scientific method, which starts by forming an idea of how the behavior of. For instance, we could suggest that the need for a product is determined by its cost. On this basis, we can conclude that if the price increases the demand decreases and if prices decrease, demand will increase. This gives us an idea that can be verified by observing the behavior. The testing of theories by examining the evidence is referred to as empirical research.

This scientific approach is clearly illustrated in the figure which is as follows:

Methodology of science

After we have made our observations, we could then

Check our theory

Reject it

Modify it in light of the evidence

3. ECONOMIC SECTION and AnalySIS

The term "economics" is employed in two major ways. One is the ability to explain and explain the performance of inflation, production, incomes, etc. However, for many, the result of these efforts is in a second goal - to increase the performance of the economy.

Therefore, we begin by trying to explain the difficulties of poverty. We could then present programs to reduce the severity of poverty. We could begin with an analysis of the ways the higher cost of energy would result in a decrease in energy consumption. Then we could decide that the nation should raise the gasoline tax.

In all cases it is the case that we first get involved in positive economics before moving on to normative economics.

Positive and Normal Economics

You might already have your own personal opinions about the kind of society that we should live in, e.g. whether it is a freedom-market "capitalist" economic system is preferable or if an "communist" economic system is more desirable. When we study economics one of the major distinctions is the distinction between a value judgement and a factual declaration.

Positive Economics is concerned with truthful statements regarding what will occur or will occur. It is limited to statements that can be confirmed through reference to actual facts e.g. What happens when a higher rate of unemployment affect inflation ? And what effect will a tax on gasoline impact the use of gasoline? An optimistic approach is more objective and more scientific, and this is the method we'll attempt to adopt in our research on economics in this article.

Normative Economics On the other hand acknowledges that in the real world most economic decisions require subjective judgments. That is that they cannot be determined only by an objective assessment of facts but rely in a certain degree on personal opinions in interpreting facts, values and ethics. There is a lot of debate about these issues but they cannot be determined by science or recourse to the evidence, e.g. should taxation take care of the wealthy to aid the less fortunate? Should the spending on defence be increased by 3 or 10 percent annually? These questions are about what should be, and are decided through a political decision.

4. PROBLEMS AND ECONOMIC GOALS

Whichever the political party that is in power the four major economic objectives are:

Control of inflation

the reduction in unemployment

Promotion of economic growth

Achieving a favorable balance of payment.

Alongside these broadly agreed-upon goals in addition to these generally agreed objectives, additional "political" economically-oriented policies could be considered, for instance an increase in income.

5. SCARCITY, CHOICE OPPORTUNITY Cost and Production Possibilities SURVEYS AND FRONTIERS

Scarcity

For the economists, everything is said to be scarce. This is because when they refer to "scarce" they simply mean "that there isn't enough items to satisfy everyone's needs until they are satisfied". The majority of people would like to own more items or things of higher quality than they do in the present. For instance, larger homes or perhaps a place to live, and better equipped with the most modern and efficient devices for labor including electric cookware, dishwashers and refrigerators; more trips to the theatre or concert hall, more travel; the newest versions of motor vehicles as well as television and radio sets as well as the majority of women display an unending desire to wear clothes. There are many desires for people however, the resources are limited.

to make the items they desire - labor and the land, the raw materials factories, buildings, and machinery which are in themselves in availability. There isn't enough productive resources on the planet, thus for the production of products and services required to satisfy the needs of everyone to the fullest extent. According to economists, every thing is always said as "scarce".

Choice and cost of opportunity

As there aren't enough resources to make all we desire There is a decision to be taken about which desires to satisfy. In the field of economics, it is believed that people will always select the option that gives the highest satisfaction. Therefore, we talk about Economic Man.

Choice is about sacrifice. If there's a choice between having guns and butter, and the country opts for guns, that is giving up butter in exchange for guns. The price of owning guns could be considered as the price that is not being in a position get butter. The price of an item by the value of what it could have of it is referred to as it's opportunity cost.

Opportunities for production and cost of opportunity

The limitations of the resources that can produce different products force society to pick between commodities that are scarce. This can be illustrated through simple arithmetic examples as well as geometrical graphs.

Consider, as an instance, that a society could invest money in two items such as butter and guns. The society's resources are constrained so there are limitations regarding the number of butter and guns that are made as evidenced through an "production potential" and "transformation curvature".

The full utilization of scarce resources is a sign of guns - the butter trade off

Alternative PRODUCTION POSSIBILITIES

POSSIBILITIES BUTTER

(Millions of pounds) (Millions of pounds)

(Thousands)

A 15

B 1 14

C 2 12

D 3 9

E 4 5

F 5 0

The above options can be visualized graphically by using the production possibility frontier. Production possibility frontiers refer to "A graphic representation of the production potential of two commodities in an economy, based on an unassailable amount of resources and the same technological environment.

Possibilities of turning Butter into gun.

Concave (to the point of origin) form of the curve comes from the assumption that resources aren't mobilized in the workplace.

Points that are not within that P.P border (to north of the North East) are unattainable using the current technological know-how. The points inside it state H. They are inefficient as resources aren't being utilized to their fullest capacity and resources aren't correctly utilized, or outdated production methods are employed.

If the production is at the edge, resources are utilized to the maximum. Production possibility curve, such as B, C and E represent the maximum production potential of both commodities.

Output G can only be considered an option for production if the capability of the nation to produce expands and the curve of production shifts upwards. This could happen if there are changes like an increasing the number of workers and the increase in stock of capital items (factories power stations transportation networks, machinery, etc.) or an increase in the technical know-how.

A few uses for the P-P Frontier

The production-possibility Frontier represented as a single curve can help introduce many of the most basic concepts of Economics.

A) For instance, Figure above is a good illustration of the definition of economics that we discussed prior to the beginning of chapter. In the chapter, we identified economics as the art of deciding what products to make. Do we need to reside in a fortress economic system filled with guns, but with modest lifestyles such as in point B in the figure 1:1? Or do we cut down the army to a mere sliver and live in an economy that is based on chocolate and butter like in Point E?. If the economy is at a level in the production potential curve, then we could declare that resources are utilized to the fullest extent and that the production than one item (guns) is not possible to produce in the absence of reduction in the other important good (butter). To allow the additional funds to be dedicated to production of guns it is necessary to have them diverted from butter production. This is a clear illustration of the fundamental concept in economics: opportunities cost.

b) The frontier of production defines the concept of scarcity. Points B, A B, C and A are viable points, given the present state of technological information and the resources available. The points to the right and over those on the border (such like G) cannot be achieved as they are not achievable without technological advancement and/or an expansion in resources available. The P-P frontier is the limit of the production of the goods.

Scarcity is the result of the reality that the P-P frontier restricts our standard of living.

c) The production-possibility schedule can also help make clear the three basic problems of economic life; What, How, and For whom to produce.

What products are made and consumed are portrayed in the place that ends up being chosen as the P.P frontier?

The way goods are manufactured requires a smart choice of techniques and the proper allocation of various amounts and types of resources that are limited to diverse industries.

Who will decide what goods will be manufactured is not clear by the P.P diagram on its own. Sometimes, however, you can speculate from it. If you come across a society that is located on the P.P frontier that has many vessels and furs, however little potatoes and small cars it is possible that it has a high degree of inequality of wealth and income among its inhabitants.

d) As a last use we could apply the logic that the frontier of P-P in the context of student life. Imagine that you only have 40 hours per week to take classes in Economics as well as Financial Accounting I. What does the P-P frontier be as for the understanding (or the grades) of Economics as well as Financial Accounting I.

OR If both commodities were grades and pleasure, what would the P-P frontier appear like? What are your current locations? Where are your lazy buddies located at the frontier?

6. THE CENTRAL Economic Problem

There are numerous economic problems that we face every day - unemployment, poverty, inflation and so on. If we employ the phrase The Economic Problem we are talking about the general issue of resource scarcity. Every society must make the most of resources that are scarce. The legendary American economics expert Paul A. Samuelson said that every economy must answer three basic questions.

What are the commodities that will be manufactured including food, clothing cars, submarines, automobiles, etc. and in what quantity?

What are the methods of producing goods? In the event the fact that we're in need of labor, land, etc., how do we use them in a way to make items and services we would like?

Who is the beneficiary of goods created? Who gets to receive the benefits of the country's products and services? To put it in another manner, how is the national product distributed among various families and individuals?

Economic systems: various solutions on the same issue

While there are many different the answers to these questions, when we examine the world, we realize that there is only a handful of ways that societies have attempted to answer these questions. These methods or strategies are known as economic systems. These are free-market, centrally planned , and mixed economies. We'll now look at these in a brief manner.

A) The free company The price system

Free market systems are in which the choice of what is produced is the result of millions of individual decisions taken by producers, consumers, and the owners of production services. The choices reflect personal preferences and desires.

To allow the free enterprise to function, it must have a pricing mechanism.

The price system is in which the most important economic decisions of the economy are made through the operation of the market price.

So, everything - homes and labour, food and land, etc. have a market price and it is because of the mechanism of market prices that we can answer the questions "What? ", "How? "", and "For who?" the decisions are made. The market is free, which creates what's known as consumer Sovereignty the state where consumers are the ultimate rulers dependent on the degree of technology, and of the type and amount of goods and services to be manufactured. The consumers are believed to exercise their power by bidding up price of the items they are most interested in and the suppliers, enthralled by the appeal of higher profits and prices make more products.

The benefits of a no-cost market system include:

1.) Ownership of the means of Production

Individuals can have the means of production i.e. capital, land, and earn income from them as interest, rent and gains.

II) Freedom of Choice and Enterprise

Entrepreneurs can invest in companies of their choice, or produce any product they want Workers are free to market their labor in the fields and occupations of their choice. consumers can consume any product that they prefer.

Iii) Self-interest as the primary motive

Businesses aim to maximize their profits, employees aim at maximising their pay and landowners strive to maximize the value of their land, and consumers aim are focused on maximizing their satisfaction

Iv) Competition

The concept of competition or economic rivalry envisions an environment wherein the marketplace for every item, there is an abundance of both sellers and buyers. It's the force of the total demand as well as supply that determine the price of the commodity, and every single participant, buyer or seller, has to consider the price to be a given because it is not under the control of any individual or influence or.

V) The price mechanism is a reliance

Price mechanism is the mechanism by which prices are determined by demand and supply as well as consumers base their budget plans, and producers' production plans on the market prices.

Price mechanism allocates limited goods and services that those who are able to afford the cost will purchase, while those who are unable to afford the cost are not able to pay.

vi) The government's role is limited

These systems aside from its primary function of providing defense, police service , and infrastructural services such as public transportation roads The Government has only a small part in direct profit-making actions.

Resource allocation in a free enterprise

Although there are no central committees organising the allocation of resources, there is supposed to be no chaos but order. The major price and allocation decisions are made in the markets. The market being the process by which the buyers and sellers of a good interact to determine its price and quantity.

If more is wanted of any commodity say wheat – a flood of new orders will be placed for it. As the buyers scramble around to buy more wheat, the sellers will raise the price of wheat to ration out a limited supply. And the higher price will cause more wheat to be produced. The reverse will also be true.

What is true of the market for commodities is also true for the markets for factors of production such as labour, land and capital inputs.

People, by being willing to spend money, signal to producers what it is they wish to be produced. Thus what things will be produced will is determined by the shilling votes of consumers, not every five years at the polls, but every day in their decisions to purchase this item and not that.

The "How?" questions is answered because one producer has to compete with others in the market; if that producer can not produce as cheaply as possible then customers will be lost to competitors. Prices are the signals for the appropriate technology.

The "for whom?" question is answered by the fact that anyone who has the money and is willing to spend it can receive the goods produced. Who has the money is determined by supply and demand in the markets for factors of production (i.e. land, labour, and capital). These markets determine the wage rates, land rents, interests rates and profits that go to make up people's incomes. The distribution of income among the population is thus determined by amounts of factors (person-hours, Acres etc.) owned and the prices of the factors (wages-rates, land-rents etc).

Advantages of a Free Market System

Incentive: People are encouraged to work hard because opportunities exist for individuals to accumulate high levels of wealth.

Choice: People can spend their money how they want; they can choose to set up their own firm or they can choose for whom they want to work.

Competition: Through competition, less efficient producers are priced out of the market; more efficient producers supply their own products at lower prices for the consumers and use factors of production more efficiently. The factors of production which are no longer needed can be used in production elsewhere. Competition also stimulates new ideas and processes, which again leads to efficient use of resources.

A free market also responds well to changes in consumer wishes, that is, it is flexible.

Because the decision happen in response to change in the market there is no need to use additional resources to make decisions, record them and check on whether or not they are being carried out. The size of the civil service is reduced.

Disadvantages of a Free Economy

The free market gives rise to certain inefficiencies called market failures i.e. where the market system fails to provide an optimal allocation of resources. These include:

Unequal distribution of wealth: The wealthier members of the society tend to hold most of the economic and political power, while the poorer members have much less influence. There is an unequal distribution of resources and sometimes production concentrates on luxuries i.e. the wants of the rich. This can lead to excessive numbers of luxury goods being produced in the economy. It may also result to social problems like crimes, corruption, etc.

Public goods: These are goods which provide benefits which are not confined to one individual household i.e. possess the characteristic of non-rival consumption and non-exclusion. The price mechanism may therefore not work efficiently to provide these services e.g. defence, education and health services.

Externalities: Since the profit motive is all important to producers, they may ignore social costs production, such as pollution. Alternatively, the market system may not reward producers whose activities have positive or beneficial effects on society.

Hardship: Although in theory factors of production such as labour are "mobile" and can be switched from one market to another, in practice this is a major problem and can lead to hardship through unemployment. It also leads to these scarce factors of production being wasted by not using them to fullest advantage.

Wasted or reduced competition: some firms may use expensive advertising campaigns to sell "new" products which are basically the same as may other products currently on sale. Other firms, who control most of the supply of some goods may choose to restrict supply and therefore keep prices artificially high; or, with other suppliers, they may agree on the prices to charge and so price will not be determined by the interaction of supply and demand.

The operation of a free market depends upon producers having the confidence that they will be able to sell what they produce. If they see the risk as being unacceptable, they will not employ resources, including labour and the general standard of living of the country will fall..

B) Planned economies

Is a system where all major economic decisions are made by a government ministry or planning organisation. Here all questions about the allocation of resources are determined by the government.

Features of this system

The command economies relies exclusively on the state. The government will decide what is made, how it is made, how much is made and how distribution takes place. The resources – factors of production – on behalf of the producers and consumers. Price levels are not determined by the forces of supply and demand but are fixed by the government.

Although division of labour and specialisation are found, the planned economies tend to be more self-sufficient and tend to take part in less international trade than market economies.

Advantages of Planned System

Uses of resources: Central planning can lead to the full use of all the factors of production, so reducing or ending unemployment.

Large scale production: Economies of scale become possible due to mass production taking place.

Public services: "Natural monopolies" such as the supply of domestic power or defence can be provided efficiently through central planning.

Basic services: There is less concentration on making luxuries for those who can afford them and greater emphasis on providing a range of goods and services for all the population.

Income distribution: There are less dramatic differences in wealth and income distribution than in market economy

Disadvantages of the Planned System

The centrally planned economies suffer from the following limitations:

Lack of choice: Consumers have little influence over what is produced and people may have little to say in what they do as a career.

Little incentive: Since competition between different producers is not as important as in the market economy, there is no great incentive to improve existing systems of production or work. Workers are given no real incentives to work harder and so production levels are not as high as they could be.

Centralised control: Because the state makes all the decisions, there must be large influential government departments. The existence of such a powerful and large bureaucracy can lead to inefficient planning and to problems of communication. Furthermore, government officials can become over privileged and use their position for personal gain, rather than for the good of the rest of the society.

The task of assessing the available resources and deciding on what to produce, how much to produce and how to produce and distribute can be too much for the central planning committee.

Also the maintenance of such a committee can be quite costly.

C) The Mixed Economy

There are no economies in the world which are entirely 'market' or planned, all will contain elements of both systems.

The degree of mix in any one economy is the result of a complex interaction of cultural, historic and political factors. For example the USA which is a typical example of a largely work-based society, but the government still plans certain areas of the economy such as defence and provides very basic care for those who cannot afford medical insurance.

Features of this system

The mixed economy includes elements of both market and planned economies. The government operates and controls the public sector, which typically consists of a range of public services such as health and education, as well as some local government services. The private sector is largely governed by the force of mechanism and "market forces", although in practice it is also controlled by various regulations and laws.

Some services may be subsidised, provided at a loss but kept for the benefit of society in general(many national railways, for example, are loss making), other services such as education or the police may be provided free of charge (though they are paid for through the taxation system).

The private sector is regulated, i.e. influenced by the price mechanism but also subject to some further government control, such as through pollution, safety and employment regulation.

Advantages of the Mixed Economy

Necessary services: are provided in a true market economy, services which were not able to make profit would not be provided.

Incentive: Since there is a private sector where individuals can make a lot of money, incentives still exist in the mixed economy.

Competition: Prices of goods and services in the private sector are kept down through competition taking place.

Disadvantages of Mixed Economy

Large monopolies can still exist in the private sector, and so competition does not really take place

There is likely to be a lot of bureaucracy and "red tape" due to existence of a public sector.

7. SPECIALIZATION AND EXCHANGE

A) Specialization

The economics of mass production upon which modern standards of living are based would not be possible if production took place in self-sufficient farm households or regions.

As such, many societies and individuals specialize or concentrate on only one activity or type of production.

Division of labour and specialisation

Division of labour refers to the situation in which the production process is split into very large number of individual operations and each operation is the special task of one worker. The workers then specialise on one activity. Four distinct stages can be distinguished in the development of division of labour and specialization.

☐ Specialisation by craft

☐ Specialisation by process

☐ Regional specialisation

☐ International division of labour

Advantages of Division of Labour

i) Greater skill of worker

The constant repetition of a task makes its performance almost automatic. The workers thus acquire greater skills at their job.

ii) A saving of time

By keeping to a single operation, a worker can accomplish a great deal more, since he wastes less time between operations. Less time, too, is required learning how to perform a single operation than to learn a complete trade.

iii) Employment of specialists

Specialisation makes it possible for each workman to specialise in the work for which he has the greatest aptitude

iv) Use of machinery

Specialisation permits the use of some tools specific to a particular task, which can make the life of a worker that much easier.

v) Less fatigue

It is sometimes claimed that the worker, habituated to the repetition of simple tasks, becomes less fatigued by his work.

Disadvantages of Division of Labour and Specialisation

i) Monotony

Doing the same work repeatedly can result in boredom, and this can offset the efficiency that would otherwise result from experience.

ii) Decline of craftsmanship

If a person does the same kind of work repeatedly according to laid down routine, he loses initiative for innovation and this can lead to loss of job satisfaction.

iii) Greater risk of unemployment

If a worker is highly specialised, he can be easily unemployed if something goes wrong with the product of his industry (e.g. if the product is found to have negative effects to health, and demands for it falls) or if a machine is introduced to perform his work.

iv) Increased interdependency

Since each worker contributes only a small part towards the completion of the final product, the efficiency and success of the whole process will depend on the efficiency and co-operation of all the workers. If some of the workers are inefficient, they can frustrate the whole system even if the rest of the workers are doing their work properly.

B) Exchange

When societies or individuals specialize, they are likely to produce a flood of "surplus" goods. They are thus bound to exchange this surplus for what they don't produce. In primitive cutlers, this exchange will take place in the form of barter. For example, it is not uncommon for food to be exchanged for weapons; or for aid in the building of a house to be exchanged for aid in cleaning a field. But exchange today in all economies – capitalist or communist takes place through he medium of money.

8. RATIONALITY

One of the most important assumptions in economics and on which much economic theory is based, is the rationality of human behaviour. In order to make predictions about human behaviour, economists assume that human behaviour is "rational" and that consumers and producers act rationally e.g. in what they will decide to buy or produce at any given price.

9. MICROECONOMICS AND MACROECONOMICS

Overall the study of economics is divided into two halves, microeconomics and macroeconomics.

"Micro"

Comes from the Greek word meaning small, and microeconomics is the study of individual economic units or particular parts of the economy e.g. how does an individual household decide to spend its income? How does an individual firm decide what volume of output to produce or what products to make? How is price of an individual product determined? How are wage levels determined in a particular industry? It thus gives a worm's eye view of the economy.

"Macro"

Comes from the Greek word meaning large, and macroeconomics is the study of "global" or collective decisions by individual households or producers. It looks at a national or international economy as a whole, e.g. Total Output, Income and Expenditure, Unemployment, Inflation Interest Rates and Balance of International Trade, etc and what economic policies a government can pursue to influence the conditions of the national economy. It thus gives a bird's eye-view of the economy.

10. CETERIS PARIBUS

The economic world is extremely complicated. There are millions of people and firms; thousands of prices and industries. One possible way of figuring out economic laws in such a setting is by controlled experiments. A controlled experiment takes place when everything else but the item under investigation is held constant. This is an essential component of scientific method.

However economists have no such luxury when testing economic laws. Therefore, when formulating economic principles economists are usually careful to state that such and such will happen, ceteris paribus which is the Latin expression meaning all other things remaining constant.

11. ECONOMIC THEORY

A body of economic principles built up as a result of logical reasoning, it provides the tools of economic analysis. It is pursued irrespective of whether it appears to be of any practical advantage or not.

12. ECONOMICS FOR ACCOUNTANTS

A few teachers and some students have questioned the rationale for including economics in a course of study for professional accountants. In order to appreciate the need for the knowledge of economics by accountants it is necessary to know something of the accountant's role. It might be necessary to provide a brief survey of accountancy before going to the value of economics to the accountant.

Accountancy

In general terms accounting consists of procedures for recording, classifying and interpreting selected experiences of an enterprise to promote effective administration. More specially, the accounting function can and often is broken down into specializations, a common distinction being made between management accounting and financial accounting. Briefly put, the role of the management accountant is to provide management with the best possible information upon which decisions can be based and enable both effective use of an organisations resources. The older specialization of cost accounting is perhaps best considered as part of management accounting which establishes budgets, standard costs and actual costs of operation and processes.

Financial accounting by contrast is concerned with the analysis, classification and recording of financial transactions in order to illustrate the effects on the performance and financial position of an undertaking. Both aspects of the accounting function must be executed if the organisation is to have adequate information for its management to formulate policy and to plan and control operations.

The role of economic knowledge

In no type of organisation can the accountant operate in isolation, however. He/she must have a working knowledge of many other areas, which impinge on the business or undertaking. The most relevant fields of knowledge are considered to be law, management, statistics, behavioural studies, information technology and economics.

The accountant is not expected to be an expert in these subject areas but to have sufficient knowledge to relate intelligently with specialists in such areas and to know enough to appreciate when and where to go for this specialist knowledge.

As part of the management team or advisor to that team, the accountant needs to appreciate the opportunities and constrains which the economic environment offers or impose on the organisation. This is true whether the organisation is in the private or public sector. All organisations must use the scarce resources available to them in an effective and efficient manner if the members of the organisations and the society generally are to gain maximum benefit. Given that allocation of resources is a central concern of economics, the relevance of economics for the accountant follows.

The accountant as a key provider of financial information for planning, control and decision making purposes will be better equipped to provide relevant information if he/she is aware of the organisational objectives, and the environmental constrains within which those objective are pursued.

As a final word one can also say that accountants need economics to understand analyse and solve economic problems of the organisation and society in general.

Chapter 10: Taxing, Spending And Borrowing

(Aka Fiscal Policy)

"The important thing for Government is not to do things which individuals are doing already, and to do them a little better or a little worse; but to do those things which at present are not done at all."

—John Maynard Keynes

Government taxing and spending sounds wild and out of control and it makes people unhappy, so, as much as possible, they refer to it as fiscal policy. Fiscal policy includes a lot of borrowing too. When the government can't tax you any more, they borrow from you (and your children, and your grandchildren, and their children). Sometimes, hopefully when the economy is booming, they even cut spending!

Taxes

This is the part where you might want to go to the gym for a round of boxing or take a bath in Sleepytime tea. If you're human, you probably at least find it mildly irritating. If you're more radical, it could inspire you to become an anarchist or a Libertarian. So sit down, put your feet up, put on some soothing music that makes you realize that money isn't everything, remember that you need those roads and highways to drive around on and want a policeman handy if someone nasty shows up at your door...and read on.

In the beginning...

Our beloved and oftentimes perverse antecedents, the Romans, came up with the first recorded taxes in western history. Of course they only used them "temporarily," usually when they wanted to invade someone else. That was fairly often though, so for all intents and purposes, Roman taxes were generally "on." Luckily for the average Roman, they didn't have eighty zillion pages of tax codes as the U.S. does. Their taxes were reasonably simple. They had the inheritance tax; a tax on auctions (like a sales tax); a tax on goods being imported, called portoria (or customs tax); and, most charmingly, a tax on slaves (folks they kidnapped from the places they invaded). Today, that tax on slaves would be called an excise tax, or commodity tax, but nowadays we generally limit it to things like fur coats and booze (more on that later).

Much of the history of taxation eerily corresponds to the history of wars. Where there's a war, there's a tax. Throughout the centuries, as in Roman times, many taxes ended when the war ended, but those days are over now that we need money to pay for exciting new missiles and missions to Mars and international diplomacy and the World Bank and fighting armed religious fanatics and building public schools and destroying toxic waste dumps and so on.

The first official income tax in the United States was created by Abraham Lincoln in 1862 to finance the Civil War. That same year, the government established the Internal Revenue Bureau, an organization of tax collectors who worked on commission. However, the vast majority of people didn't bother to file tax returns.

In 1913, Congress passed the 16th Amendment, the advent of the permanent income tax. And, even though the tax collectors no longer work on commission, there's none of this "Gosh, maybe I'll file and maybe I won't." You're gonna pay, whether you feel like it or not.

Federal and state income tax

The lion's share of government income today comes from individual income tax, that nasty chunk of money taken out of your pay check every week. Together, individual Americans fork over about 42% of the government's income.

The amount you pay depends on which "tax bracket" you're in. Your tax bracket is based on how much money you make, plus your living situation (married, single, widowed, head of household—which means you have dependents living with you—or married filing separately). Basically, the more you make, the higher percentage you pay, which is referred to as "progressive taxation." The design of tax brackets has changed several times over the years, depending on who is in power. In 1999, the tax rates for a single person looked roughly like this:

$0 to $25,749 = 15%.

$25,750 to $62,449 = 28%.

$62,450 to $130,249 = 31%.

$130,250 to $283,149 = 36%.

$283,150 and more = 39.6%.

After the tax cuts passed under President Bush, it looked like this:

Up to $8,500 = 10%

$8,501 to $34,500 = 15%

$34,501 to $83,600 = 25%

$83,601 to $174,400 = 28%

$174,401 to $379,150 = 33%

$379,151 or more = 35%

You might conclude from these numbers that it doesn't pay to earn a bigger salary or that a raise might end up costing you more. Luckily, that's not so. Say you're single and making $23,000. Under 1999 tax rates, you'll pay 15% of the $23,000. Then you get a $10,000 raise, which adds up to $33,000, which puts you in the 28% bracket. You'll actually only pay 28% on the amount between $25,750 and $33,000. In other words, even if you're in the 28% bracket, you don't pay 28% on the full amount.

One thing about the Federal income tax law that traditionally makes a lot of people angry is referred to as the "marriage penalty." Married couples where both are working pay higher taxes than they would if they weren't married. However, if only one partner in the couple is working, or if the second partner doesn't make much, the tax breaks are magnificent. In other words, the tax law is set up to benefit the "traditional" marriage (with one stay-at-home partner). This law was under fire for years and was removed from the tax code under the Bush tax cuts. As of this writing, the marriage penalty is scheduled to return in 2013.

Most states also charge an individual income tax. Each state has its own scheme and its own tax brackets, often more brackets than the Feds. If you're thinking about moving because of high state income taxes, states that don't charge income tax are Alaska, Florida, Nevada, New Hampshire, South Dakota, Tennessee, Texas, Washington, and Wyoming.

The government uses several methods to trick you into thinking they aren't so greedy after all. They give you "personal exemptions." These are amounts that you deduct from your taxable income. For example, if you're single, you get one personal exemption, say $3,800 (2012). So, if your income is $40,000, you get taxed on $36,200. If you're married, filing jointly, with a couple kids, you get to deduct dependent exemptions.

There's also the "deduction" (as opposed to the obviously different "exemption"). You can take a standard deduction or itemized deduction. If you don't own a house or a business, you will usually take the standard deduction. That's generally a fixed amount that you subtract from your gross income (your income before taxes). The amount varies depending on how many people are in your household. Your reward for doing this is you get to fill out the "easy" tax form.

On the other hand, you may have a lot of write-offs. A write-off is something you can deduct from your income, such as interest on your home loan (called mortgage interest), medical expenses, or personal business expenses (if you run your own business out of your home). This is called itemizing your deductions, and your punishment is you have to fill out a bunch of nasty forms which you probably won't be able to figure out. (The IRS once estimated that it takes an average of 653 minutes, or almost 11 hours, to fill out these forms.)

Then, when you're finished filling out the Federal forms, you get to fill out the state income tax form. To keep you from killing yourself, there's a bit of candy some state governments might allow you, called a "credit." This is an amount of money you deduct from your actual tax amount. For example, some states have the "renter's credit," which means you get to deduct a certain amount from your tax bill if you're a renter.

There's also the "low-income credit." That means if your income is below a certain amount you get to deduct a certain amount from your income, usually per household member. Another credit is the "child credit" which allows low-income families to deduct a certain amount per child.

The point of these credits is to reduce the tax burden on the lowest income citizens. However, one of the biggest advantages of having a high income is that you also tend to have a lot of write-offs. The wealthiest citizens often end up having so many write-offs that their tax rate ends up being the same or lower than that paid by the lowest income citizens. That is, they might have a gross income of five million dollars but their net income (after write-offs) is five thousand dollars.

Corporate income taxes

Corporate income taxes account for about 9% of the government's income. Sure, it seems like that should just about cover one CEO's share (the highest paid U.S. CEO in 2012 was McKesson CEO John Hammergren, who made over $131 million for the year, according to Forbes), but you've heard about all those big tax write-offs that corporations get. Corporations can deduct just about everything from their taxable income, including everyone's salaries, rent, paper clips, donuts in the coffee room, travel expenses, depreciation (wear and tear), paintings of "Elk in the Rockies" for the Vice President's office, plus martinis and bikini girls for those offsite corporate retreats. All this money comes off the top, or put the official way, it is deducted from the gross income. Gross income is the total amount of income, before expenses. After Corporation XYZ subtracts their deductions, they come up with their taxable income, which sometimes, amazingly, magically, comes out to zero, which means they don't pay any corporate income taxes. These miraculous numbers can even add up to a loss, which they can then carry forward to the next tax year.

Property taxes

A property tax is a tax on anything you own that can be considered your property or wealth. For centuries, property taxes played a bigger role in financing the government than they do today. (The individual income tax is now the big cash cow). Early property taxes were collected on livestock such as horses and cattle; on agricultural products such as fruits, grains, vegetables; on capital assets—things you own that are worth money such as homes, buggies, equipment.

Today, the term "property" applies to your land, house, car, speedboat; also, investments (stocks and bonds), even cash in the bank. For most people, property tax means a tax on your house, if you own one. This is almost always a local tax, meaning it's collected by the city or county government where you live. The tax is generally paid in a lump sum, which is why people grumble about it more than sales tax or income tax. If you're still paying off your mortgage (the money you borrowed to buy your house), the property tax is usually folded into those monthly payments.

Property tax rates vary widely from county to county. In one county, the property tax might be 1.25% of the purchase price of your home, paid annually. So, if your house is assessed at a value of $100,000, every year you pay the local government $1,250 in property taxes. In the next county over, the rate might be .09% so you only pay $900 for the same house. The property tax guy (called an "assessor") might also decide your house is worth more (aka, increase your assessment), based on what's going on in the real estate market around you. You could suddenly find yourself paying 1.25% of $150,000. This gets people upset too, and there have been several "property tax revolts" in various states.

Property owners hate this tax. There are usually no deductions or credits; there's hardly any way out of it, though some counties allow a senior citizen's discount. If you're determined, perhaps you could buy a red Corvette for the tax guy or tie up a high assessment in appeals court.

The government loves this tax because it's a reliable income. If the economy slows down, the amount of property tax the government collects usually doesn't go down with it, like sales and income tax revenues do. Advocates for the poor like property taxes because most poor people are renters and don't pay property tax—at least not directly. Folks with children should love the property tax because it's generally used to pay for the public schools in your neighborhood. A hefty chunk of it also goes for police and the fire department, plus street maintenance.

Social Security and Medicare tax

Social Security in the United States was created in 1935 by Franklin D. Roosevelt to serve as the country's "retirement fund." Each person would pay a percentage of their income into this fund. The government would invest it, and at retirement, each person would collect a monthly check out of the fund.

Social Security tax accounts for about 34% of government income, though it's not really there for the government to spend on anything except benefits. (Sometimes the government cheats and borrows from this fund). This is that other chunk of money that disappears from your paycheck. Right now, the Social Security tax is 10.4% (more than half of which is paid by your employer, unless you're self-employed).

This is the part where you might get a little annoyed: Social Security is supposed to pay for your golden years, but the money is being used to pay today's bills. The retirement age is gradually being raised, a process that began back in the year 2000. Not only that, but rumor has it the tax will have to increase to 18% to keep the Social Security system going. Why? There is an enormous mass of aging people called "baby boomers" who are starting to collect Social Security. Soon, there will be a lot more 65-year-olds collecting benefits than 35-year-olds paying into the fund. The money that the baby boomers are paying in now is all being spent on the people who are already retired. So, when these millions of baby boomers are collecting, the system will be supported by the people working at that time.

The Medicare tax is about 1.4 percent of your income, and goes into a great pool that is used to cover senior citizen's medical expenses. There is also a lot of concern about the stability of the Medicare fund. Since the only people on Medicare are the elderly, expenses per person tend to be very high.

Sales tax

The sales tax is a percentage added to your bill when you buy your groceries, stereos, McDonald's hamburgers—everything. This is a state tax, and can be anywhere between 7% in states like Mississippi and Rhode Island to zero percent in others such as Delaware and New Hampshire. The city and county where you live will probably get in on the act too, with their own taxes.

Capital gains tax

This is a tax on income that you earn from investments. You have to pay capital gains tax whenever there's an increase in the value of your capital assets, like stocks, bonds, or mutual funds. For example, say you bought stock last year for $100,000, and this year it's worth $150,000. That extra $50,000 is considered "capital gains" and you have to pay taxes on it. (You don't get a refund if it goes down though.)

The Federal taxes on this are different depending on how long you owned the asset, what type of capital it was, and what your income bracket is. The capital gains tax is generally lower than income tax.

Inheritance tax and estate tax

Inheritance tax is what you pay when a family member dies and leaves money or property to you. The state government wants a cut of that. The Federal government wants a chunk too, only they call it the estate tax (maybe so you don't feel like you're paying the same tax twice, which you are). As of 1997, the Feds allowed a $600,000 exemption. That amount has increased every year since and as of 2012, it was $5.5 million. So, unless your relative is leaving you an enormous fortune, you won't have to pay the "estate" tax. Many state laws don't provide the exemption. In Massachusetts for example, it's 18% off the top, no matter how much the amount. In other states, if you're the "lineal heir" (a son or daughter) you get exemptions, but if you're a cousin for example, you pay a huge percentage. Other states have no inheritance tax.

The original idea behind this tax was to avoid creating an aristocracy, that evil thing we fought our American revolution to get rid of. Now that we do have an American aristocracy, the inheritance and estate taxes are just another form of income for the government.

In some places you can avoid these taxes by giving "gifts" (wads of money) to your heirs before you die. But then you might have to pay the "gift tax" (see "Gift taxes").

Excise or commodity tax

Excise, or commodity taxes are taxes on the production, sale, or consumption of commodities. A commodity is a "non-essential" good, such as whiskey or cigarettes. The commodity tax is charged only for these "special" goods, as opposed to the sales tax, which you pay no matter what you're buying.

Excise tax is the same thing—a tax on a commodity. To clarify this, the roots of the word "excise" refer to "cutting," as in, for example, taking a cut from your money.

Tax collectors have been very creative indeed about collecting excise and commodity taxes. History shows us that there have taxes on birth, marriage, death, and everything that falls between. This includes gloves, hats, tea, stamps, hair powder, medicine, hearths, malt, salt, soap, windows, glass, leather, coal, paper, candles, hops, booze, gasoline, fur coats, yachts, hunting, driving, homes, cars, food, flying, and cigarettes. If they can find a way to tax it, they will.

These taxes provide the government with a unique power to go after a certain segment of society. Commodity taxes are often used to discourage good citizens from doing naughty things like drinking and smoking. They are sometimes referred to as "sin taxes" or "luxury taxes."

Take smokers, for example. In 2009, the Feds raised the cigarette tax to $1.01 per pack, which hopefully prompted millions of people to quit smoking. Most states also tax cigarettes. Not only that, when governments began taxing cigarettes heavily, the tobacco companies made up for the loss of smokers by increasing the cost of cigarettes as well, which makes a pack very expensive indeed.

Drinkers fare a bit better than smokers. Federal taxes on beer are about seven percent. And how about gasoline? The Feds are taking more than 18 cents a gallon, while the states are taking anywhere from 7 to 36 cents per gallon. This means that an average of 43 cents per gallon of gas is going for taxes.

Land use tax

Another early form of "property tax" that is still widely in use in the western U.S. is the land use tax. The government owns much of the land in the west, and it charges people for using it. For example, western cattlemen pay a fee to the government for grazing their herds on government lands.

Taxes on interest

If you have money in the bank and you collect interest on it, the government wants a cut of that too.

Gift taxes

One way of avoiding inheritance taxes is to "gift" money to your heirs before you die. You can give up to $13,000, per person, per year before it becomes taxable. A problem most of us don't have to worry about.

Ways to avoid taxes

After all that good news, here's the bad news: there isn't a whole lot you can do to avoid taxes. Corporations and rich people have more options, and some schemes are more legitimate than others.

If your company is involved in international trade, you can incorporate in a tax haven country, such as Bahamas, Cayman Islands, Isle of Man, Ireland, Cook Islands, Panama, Vanuatu, Nevis, and many others. This type of incorporation is referred as "offshore." It can cost you anywhere from $500 to $10,000 to set up, and it's debatable how much you can save in taxes. You have to research the laws of each country to determine which haven would best benefit your tax situation. Of course, there are many financial companies who will handle it for you, along with certain tax attorneys. An attorney is more expensive but might be a wiser choice. Using a tax haven to avoid taxation isn't considered quite squeaky clean and all-American, and if you're not careful, you could find yourself just on the other side of "legal," and riding a minivan to jail. Even if you are legal, it's still not considered entirely patriotic, and politicians who engage in this behavior generally don't get a lot of love from voters. Although many otherwise legitimate companies incorporate in offshore countries to ease their tax bills, tax havens are also used by criminals to launder money. Money laundering refers to taking "dirty" money, such as money earned selling drugs, and moving it through the accounts of more legitimate businesses. At the end of the process the money appears to have been earned through legal business activities.

Swiss bank accounts are popular spots for "hiding" money because Swiss banking laws call for extreme secrecy. In most countries, police and government officials (such as IRS officers) are allowed to see your banking records if they ask. Swiss bankers historically wouldn't let anyone see your banking records, no matter who asked. You could also keep your name out of it altogether by getting a "numbered" Swiss account, which is an account identified only by number. To get a Swiss bank account, you need "legitimate funds," and a minimum of $250,000. You will also draw immediate suspicion toward yourself just by opening an account, even if you're doing it because your grandmother was from Switzerland and you're planning to retire to the family chalet. In recent years, a number of governments have been challenging the secrecy of Swiss banks. Some of these efforts have been successful and Swiss banks have started releasing names. As a result, thousands of people with formerly secret Swiss bank accounts are now under investigation for tax evasion.

The most typical (and legal) options you have to avoid taxes are the tax shelter and the write-off.

A tax shelter is a "shelter" for your money. For corporations or investors with lots of money to protect, a tax shelter might be a certain type of investment designed to save money based on current tax laws. Cattle companies and real estate investments were each popular for a while.

For working folks, a shelter usually means a special type of account with an investment firm. What's special about these accounts is that the money you put in is "pre-tax" money, meaning it comes out of your gross income. (Gross income is the total amount of your income; net income is the amount of your income after taxes.) In other words, you don't need to pay taxes on the money—at least not right now.

The most common types are Individual Retirement Accounts (IRAs) and 401k plans. IRAs are generally opened by individuals; 401k plans are usually offered by employers (who sometimes match your contributions up to a certain limit). The money is then invested in various stocks, bonds, and mutual funds. The trick is, you have to promise not to touch the money until you reach retirement age. If you take it out before you retire (referred to as "early withdrawal"), you have to pay a penalty—often 10% of the amount—plus taxes. There are some exceptions for people with disabilities and early retirement.

The government puts a limit on how much you can put aside in these "sheltered" accounts—say, $5,000 per year.

Another method of avoiding taxes is using tax write-offs. A write-off is an expense that you had to pay in order to conduct your business. In the case of a corporation, nearly everything it spends is an "expense," so corporate accountants have a field day with write-offs. For individuals, it's a bit more tricky. If you're running a small business out of your home, you can write off quite a few things, like a percentage of your rent or mortgage, the cost of your computer and monthly internet fees. However, even the kinder, gentler IRS likes to nail people who try to stretch the limits of these write-offs, so watch out. If you're a regular employee of some company, just about the only major thing you can write off is the mortgage on your home, if you own one. You also get to deduct last year's state taxes and licensing fees that you paid, just so it doesn't look like you're being taxed twice on the same money (though you are, by way of sales and commodity taxes).

You can always become a tax protestor, though you'll probably end up in jail or exile. The first renowned tax protestor was the 11th Century Anglo-Saxon (early Britain) woman, Lady Godiva, who was also an early example of "smart women who choose extremely horrible men." Her husband, an Earl who had a strange sense of humor, agreed to lower his nasty taxes on the population if his wife would ride naked around town on her horse. So, the legend goes, she did and he did. (This is also where we got the term "Peeping Tom," named after the town nitwit who reportedly peeped and turned blind).

Conclusion

I want to thank you again for taking the time and reading this book.

I hope this book was able to help you understand economics and what it actually means. Economy is a huge part of our life. We may not like it, but that is the truth. Every change of economic activity in the economic market of the world and of our country can have a significant effect on our life. Financial crisis may cost us our job, or result in our inability to enroll into college, or the inability to provide for one's family.

However, looking up economics basics online is a difficult task. First, online pages are the number one source of incorrect information. Second, when you try to look something up on reliable pages, you get results that are hard to understand.

This book gave you all about the information you need about the market, economy, money, and trading in a way that combined both simplicity and reliable information.

The purpose of the book wasn't just to teach you about economy and the market in general. The ideas of this book can be implemented into your own business or help you understand the business and economy itself before you establish your own company or small business.

In addition, understanding how economy works prepares you for all challenges that can arise later in life.